Suffer The Children

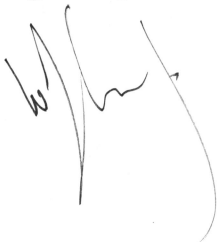

W. J. THOMPSON, JR.

FIRST EDITION

ISBN: 978-1-939748-46-1

Library of Congress Control Number: 2014932749

Published by

P.O. Box 2839, Apopka, FL 32704

Printed in the United States of America

Disclaimer: The views and opinions expressed in this book are solely those of the authors and other contributors. These views and opinions do not necessarily represent those of Certa Publishing.

Table of Contents

Dedication

to

Marilyn, Rebecca J., Annie Z. & Charlotte

Introduction

The message of the Bible is as relevant today as it has been for centuries in addressing the nature of the relationship God desires for his most vulnerable creation: children. The most precious gift from God outside of God's inspiration is to have the responsibility of caring for, facilitating and nurturing the life and destiny of a child. In the accounts recorded by historic, poetic, prophetic, gospel and apostolic authors lie the secret treasures of the treatment of children, who always find favor and freedom in the presence of a caring and tender God.

As a young preacher, sharing this message at youth conferences, youth revivals, annual youth days, lock-ins, juvenile detention centers, college campuses and youth festivals across the United States, Africa, Australia, Canada and the Caribbean, and then blessed with the opportunity to serve as a youth minister and youth and young adult pastor, I have developed a collection of messages called, "Suffer the Children."

Some messages were developed on college campuses, some on mission trips and some in the church van. I might also add that many were developed right after youth and young adult choir rehearsals and Christmas and Easter production rehearsals, with hay and straw in my socks and glue and Crayola under my fingernails. Some were developed in isolation and others in the heat of group discussions, even after a long afternoon at Six Flags America, a Magic Johnson Theatre and a knock on my dorm room door in Carver and Drew Halls on the campus of Howard University.

Some of these presentations emerged in the heat of crisis, or right after I got a call from a child afraid to call home with disappointing news and others at the graduation ceremony of a child needing multiple hours of positive academic reinforcement and a comeback from being held back three years in a row, due to lack of meeting promotion requirements. One in particular emerged right after a parent left my Columbia office needing to know, "What does God say to parents with growing children?"

In these pages, you will experience the journey of a young preacher trying to grapple with a call to share a message of hope and triumph with and to serve a generation he is a part of.

Jesus clearly expresses the thought that the kingdom belongs to those who come as little children. And with the word "suffer" preceding the phrase, the message literally invites any hindrances to aggressively move, giving the children free access and a central seat in the hearing and carrying out of the kingdom agenda.

May you find inspiration, accountability and revelation in these next few pages that will assist you in creating a path for the children to encounter the kingdom.

CHAPTER ONE

A Child's Defense

Focal Passage: Mark 9:35-46 (Living Bible)

³⁵ He sat down and called them around him and said, "Anyone wanting to be the greatest must be the least—the servant of all!" ³⁶ Then he placed a little child among them; and taking the child in his arms he said to them, ³⁷ "Anyone who welcomes a little child like this in my name is welcoming me, and anyone who welcomes me is welcoming my Father who sent me!" ³⁸ One of his disciples, John, told him one day, "Teacher, we saw a man using your name to cast out demons; but we told him not to, for he isn't one of our group." ³⁹ "Don't forbid him!" Jesus said. "For no one doing miracles in my name will quickly turn against me. ⁴⁰ Anyone who isn't against us is for us. ⁴¹ If anyone so much as gives you a cup of water because you are Christ's —I say this solemnly—he won't lose his reward. ⁴² But if someone causes one of these little ones who believe in me to lose faith—it would be better for that man if a huge millstone were tied around his neck and he were thrown into the sea. [43-44] *"If your hand does wrong, cut it off. Better live forever with one hand than be thrown into the unquenchable fires of hell with two!* [45-46] *If your foot carries you toward evil, cut it off! Better be lame and live forever than have two feet that carry you to hell.*

Are you aware of the many acts of violence against children that are currently taking place around the world? According to *Prison Bound: The Denial of Juvenile Justice in Pakistan*, in May of 1998, a 13-year-old boy named, Ghulam Jilani, died just hours after he was arrested and taken to a police station in Mansehra. Though officially reported as a homicide, an eye-witness arrested with Jilani indicated that he died after severe prolonged torture. The autopsy report stated that Jilani had died of head injuries. The other boy, Jilani's eye-witness, had also been physically abused while in custody.

Did you know that street children in Kenya also reported abuse during interrogations? It is said that policemen whipped them with cable cords when they were questioned concerning the location of their parents.

Have you heard that in Jamaica, a 16-year-old boy accused of stealing money was brought to a police station, where he was beaten with an electrical cord, both in his cell and in the guard room?

According to the periodical *United States: Modern*

Capital of Human Rights, children in juvenile detention centers in Georgia were bound to a bed by their wrists and ankles for several hours, often face down, as a form of discipline. And in some Colorado juvenile detention centers, attacks and sexual assaults on residents were described as routine events.

In Baltimore City Detention Centers, guards sometimes allow youths to fight with each other in what is called the "square dance." F. Jackson records in the book, *No Minor Matter: Children in Maryland Jails*, that the "square dance" ends with busted heads, slashes over eyes, broken fingers, cut lips and maybe a broken nose. But the injured don't go to the hospital for treatment.

In another Maryland jail, a 17-year-old reported adult inmates in his section continually harassed him by throwing urine and excrement into his cell.

There is even violence in schools. Human Rights Watch found that in the United States, children are often victimized because of their sexual orientation and gender identity. According to their 2008 report on child violence in schools, "Lesbian, gay, bisexual and transgender youths who attend public schools were relentlessly harassed and sometimes physically attacked. They were kicked, spit on, cut with knives, strangled, thrown against lockers and dragged down a flight of stairs."

In at least 65 countries, corporal punishment is permitted as a method of discipline. According to the Global Initiative to End All Corporal Punishment of Children, children may be spanked, slapped, caned, strapped or beaten as a result of misbehavior, poor academic performance or sometimes for no reason at all.

In a letter shared with project *Juvenile In Justice*, a 13-year-old girl in Johannesburg left school, not because she wanted to abandon her education, but because she was gang raped by male classmates and felt unsafe while the boys remained there.

There are even acts of violence against children in orphanages. In some cases, according to *Abandoned to the State,* adult staff members in orphanages sometimes strike and humiliate children. This report also revealed that some of the punishments included: forcing a smaller child into a small wooden chest to be thrown out of a window or holding a smaller child upside down out of a window. Reports also revealed that some children were electrocuted, some had their heads shoved into a toilet, some boys had their testicles squeezed during interrogation and some were locked in freezers.

In some places like Sierra Leone, children have been murdered, tortured, beaten, raped and enslaved for sexual purposes. In the Democratic Republic of the Congo, thousands of children have been recruited by government forces, militias and rebel forces. They were beaten, ill-treated and used as cannon fodder. Some were trained to shoot and became casualties of war.

In Polk County, Florida, eight teenagers beat a 16-year-old girl up and put the video on the web. They thought nothing of what they had done and expressed no remorse. In another instance, a mother taught her children how to steal from J.C. Penny, and yet another shopped online while her child drowned in a tub filled with water. Being forced to assume adult responsibilities, due to a parental addiction to narcotics, works and hopelessness, has violated many of our children. Many children have to grow up with a silent or absent father or a mother who is possessive or depressed because of the absent father and controls the child because he or she can't control his or her mate. So many acts of violence are perpetrated against the little ones, the powerless and the vulnerable!

There are even acts of violence against children in religious sects. Yes, even in the church! Fondling fathers destroy the innocence of sacred sons. Pedophilic priests pervert the prayers of passionate parishioners. Deacons corner damsels and dare them to expose themselves. Polygamist patriarchs and self-proclaimed procreation prophets on ranches in Texas marry young girls as soon as they reach puberty. These are acts of violence against the powerless and vulnerable. In his research on *Satanism, Sexual Abuse and the Church,* Dr. Gregory Ried reports that 70% of the sexual abuse against children and adolescents has taken place, if not *in* church settings, then with Christians who were in a position to do something and did nothing at all. This violence is happening in situations where love, embrace, trust, healing and wholeness are the mega-themes of the institution. In all of these situations, children are being violated, taken advantage of and abused. When will someone present a defense on behalf of the children?

I agree with Human Rights Watch and their recommendations to authorities to deal with these situations. So, of course, we need to investigate violence against children in correctional and detention centers. And we need to institute training programs in the handling and treating of children and their basic rights. And we need to make sure children understand their rights. We should establish effective and confidential complaint mechanisms. We must not allow children to share correctional facilities with adults. We must abolish corporal punishment in schools. We must investigate police brutality and roundups of children. We must establish independent complaint boards.

We must prohibit sexual violence, harassment and other sexual misconduct in schools. We must endorse legislation to protect students from harassment and discrimination on the basis of sexual orientation and gender identity. We must scrutinize incidents of abuse of children in orphanages and bring to justice their predators. We have to shield children from being recruited as soldiers, and ensure their protection in refugee camps.

We must teach our children that everybody who smiles in their face is not their friend. We must let them know that some people are predators and act irresponsibly. It is our job to provide a defense for the children.

But, along with that, we must share John Marks' declaration for powerless dependents. Written around 70 CE, to a group of disciples, who were praying for power, it states,

"And if anyone offend, one of these little ones who believes in Me, it would be better for him to be thrown into the sea with a millstone tied around his neck." (Mark 9:42 KJV)

Jesus becomes the protector of the powerless and the vindicator of the vulnerable. The Greek word here for offend is *scandalize*, which means to "cause to sin, cause to fall in sin or to entrap or entice and to go astray." When we perpetuate the aforementioned institutions, we become the "anyone." When we see this violence and remain silent we become the "anyone." When we initiate this violence from our positions of influence, we become the "anyone." And this text invites those "anyones" to become entangled with a millstone and be thrown into the sea.

Jesus teaches the disciples who desire positional power, influence, rank and responsibility to be caring. Implying that we must be looked upon as the least of them to be the looked upon as the greatest among them. A child was called to His side and became the illustration of those who follow Christ; He must be concerned for all, even the lowest of this society. In following Christ, there must be a concern for those devalued and disenfranchised.

Jesus teaches the disciples to be careful, for with the same power to lead comes the ability to mislead. Be careful in your conduct, be meticulous in your manners, be provident in your posture, be disciplined in your demeanor and be watchful in your ways.

Lastly, Jesus shares with His disciples the call to be Christ-like, to live in peace with one another. Be the peacemaker. When the uproar happens, find your place of tranquility. Instead of bad blood, promote brotherhood. Instead of agitation, build fraternization and instead of violence, choose the non-violent approach.

As followers of Christ we must be caring, careful and Christ-like. It is the child's only defense.

CHAPTER TWO

A Child's Revival

Focal Passage: Luke 8:40-56

⁴⁰ So it was, when Jesus returned, that the multitude welcomed Him, for they were all waiting for Him. ⁴¹ And behold, there came a man named Jairus, and he was a ruler of the synagogue. And he fell down at Jesus' feet and begged Him to come to his house, ⁴² for he had an only daughter about twelve years of age, and she was dying. But as He went, the multitudes thronged Him. ⁴³ Now a woman, having a flow of blood for twelve years, who had spent all her livelihood on physicians and could not be healed by any, ⁴⁴ came from behind and touched the border of His garment. And immediately her flow of blood stopped. ⁴⁵ And Jesus said, "Who touched Me?" When all denied it, Peter and those with him said, "Master, the multitudes throng and press You, and You say, 'Who touched Me?'" ⁴⁶ But Jesus said, "Somebody touched Me, for I perceived power going out from Me." ⁴⁷ Now when the woman saw that she was not hidden, she came trembling; and falling down before Him, she declared to Him in the presence of all the people the reason she had touched Him and how she was healed immediately. ⁴⁸ And He said to her, "Daughter, be of good cheer; your faith has made you well. Go in peace." ⁴⁹ While He was still speaking, someone came from the ruler of the synagogue's house, saying to him, "Your daughter is dead. Do not trouble the Teacher." ⁵⁰ But when Jesus heard it, He answered him, saying, "Do not be afraid; only believe, and she will be made well." ⁵¹ When He came into the house, He permitted no one to go in except Peter, James, and John, and the father and mother of the girl. ⁵² Now all wept and mourned for her; but He said, "Do not weep; she is not dead, but sleeping." ⁵³ And they ridiculed Him, knowing that she was dead. ⁵⁴ But He put them all outside, took her by the hand and called, saying, "Little girl, arise." ⁵⁵ Then her spirit returned, and she arose immediately. And He commanded that she be given something to eat. ⁵⁶ And her parents were astonished, but He charged them to tell no one what had happened.

Believe it or not, there have been more acts of violence committed against children these past two years then I have ever seen in my life. Children are committing acts of violence against children. Parents are committing acts of violence against children. The Hip Hop culture is committing acts of violence against children. Reality TV shows are committing acts of violence against children. Uncontrolled police officials are committing acts of violence against children. School administrators are committing acts of violence against children. Even churches are committing acts of violence against children. And the children are in trouble.

You may not agree, but if you are a parent and you leave your child in the bathtub while shopping online and they are injured, you are committing an act of violence against a child. If you have a little brother or sister and you lock them in the closet, pull their hair, hide their toys or tell them lies, you are committing an act of violence against them. If you are a parent and you leave your child with nasty neighbors, cursing cousins, bad babysitters, dead-beat dads or an under-aged adolescent, you are committing an act of violence. The children are in trouble.

If you are a representative of the Hip Hop culture and you sell your albums instructing young people to commit acts of violence against themselves and others, you are committing an act of violence. If you solicit sex in a club and don't care who's watching, you are committing an act of violence. If you call yourself, Black Entertainment Television (BET), and your hottest shows display little girls half-naked, brothers costumed with bling and you teach children to "Walk it Out" rather than to spell correctly, you are committing an act of violence. If you are a network that teaches young people mindless behavior, to become a Chief Keef (17-year-old) or Soulja Boy or Girl but not to become a student of higher education, you are committing an act of violence. If 106 & Park (one-O-six and Park) is the best representation of African American culture you have to offer, you are committing an act of violence. If you promote, "lick it like a lollipop, as you hear the beat drop," you are committing an act of violence. If you are a police officer that man-handles teenage girls as if they are men because they missed curfew, you are committing an act of violence.

When you force pretty princesses, who have yet to reach puberty, to be married, mastered and eternally mutilated by portraying yourself as a prophetic, polygamist (patriarch), you are committing an act of violence. If you ride up and down neighborhood streets in your Jaguar, scoping out little girls to be your next victim, you are committing an act of violence. And the children are in trouble.

If you are a school administrator or a substitute teacher that chases and tackles a student in the hall, you are committing an act of violence. If you are a school system run over by gang violence, perpetuating bully activity like you don't see it or you are allowing the TV's to teach and not the teachers, you are committing an act of violence. The children are in trouble.

If you are a church and you don't make room for the children to express themselves or teach them how to live an authentic life that pleases God, but instead force them to sing, usher, and come to youth revivals, you are committing an act of violence. And the children are in trouble.

If you distract a child while I preach with your new cell

phone, I-pod, I-pad, PS2, MP3, text messaging or pass funny notes, checking out the girl across the way, or even attempt to calculate when service will be over, you are committing an act of violence. And the children are in trouble.

In our text, Luke invites us to the story of a child in trouble. Not only is this child in trouble, but the text lets us know that she is near death.

This 12-year-old little girl is a powerful religious leader's daughter. She has been raised up around the temple, watching her father handle church responsibilities and has walked with the great teachers of the law. She is used to being around people with prestige, power and promise. However, right before she has the opportunity to fulfill her God-given destiny, her plan to move out and ahead or her dreams of womanhood and beginning family life, her life is snatched from her by an illness that leaves her at the point of death. Have you ever encountered something so traumatic that it's almost killed you? Have you ever been so close to something so good that you could smell it only to have something come along and knock you off track like never before? Have you ever been so close to moving on and moving forward only to have a situation knock you off your focus, your passion and your vision? Have you ever been so close to reaching a breakthrough to your future, or to your deliverance, only to have something happens that almost takes you out? This little girl was in trouble. She was at the point of death, at the point of no return, at the place between time and eternity. She was in trouble. And not only did she know she was in trouble, her father knew she was in trouble. Her father saw that opportunity was being snatched from her and had to find a revival for his child. He had to find somebody who could help her, somebody who could reverse this curse, and remove the thing that was taking his child. He needed a child's revival.

Have you ever been in a place where you saw somebody in trouble and could not help them? Nothing hurts a mother like a son slipping into harms way and she can't help him. Nothing hurts a father like a daughter distracted from destiny and he can't save her. He saw his daughter, he saw her situation and he saw death knocking at her door. He saw her helplessness. He needed revival for his child.

In order to revive a child I would like to suggest that you need a concerned parent. You need somebody that is concerned about you. You need somebody that can lead and guide you. You need somebody that can do more than pay child support. Even if they are not your real parents, you need a guardian. You need somebody to watch over you, and show you the warning signs and someone to be the example for you. TI is not concerned, Nelly is not concerned, Lil Wayne is not concerned, 50 cent can't buy anything and he is not concerned. You need a concerned parent. Shawty Lo and all of his Baby Momma's kids need a parent. Kim Kardashian needs a parent. Foxy Brown needs a parent. Snoop Doggy Dog, Cherish, Busta Rhymes and Rick Ross all need somebody. Even Olivia Pope, from Scandal, called out, "Dad," during a recent show.

You need somebody that is concerned. You might think you are grown, feel like you are grown and look like you are grown, but you still need somebody. You need somebody that can see your future and know that life for you is not over. You need somebody that has sense enough to find you some help rather than support your habit. We all need a concerned parent.

Secondly, I suggest in order to revive a child you need a sympathetic Savior. When Jesus hears about the situation, His heart immediately reroutes its agenda and moves toward the cry of the concerned parent of a child that is near death. Even though interrupted by the healing of a woman who had issues for 12 years, and receiving word that the child is dead, Jesus still came to the child's rescue. You need a Savior, somebody that will be interrupted but will still keep coming. You need a sympathetic Savior who will tell the concerned parent, "Do not be afraid, only believe." You better ask God to save your parents.

You need a Savior that can hear the cry of a parent and still keep coming to your rescue. Momma, don't buy me stuff, pray for me. Daddy don't ignore the signs, talk to Jesus about me. You need a sympathetic Savior, a Savior that comes on the scene and smells death but still sees life. A Savior who will not listen to what everyone else is saying about your condition, but will help you. A sympathetic Savior that will dismiss the crowd, take your momma and daddy, the power of Peter and the compassion and wisdom of John and shut the door and deal with you. You need a sympathetic Savior that will ignore the laughs and see the joy that is about to come back into your life.

You need a sympathetic Savior that will call you back to life. And I suggest counseling, but the name of Jesus still works. And I promote after-school programs, but Jesus has power to change. And I promote support groups, but the name of the Lord is a strong tower, and the righteous can run into it and be saved. A life with Jesus can handle bullies. A life with Jesus can handle peer pressure. A life with Jesus can get you through dead situations. A life with Jesus can get you through the "hood" mentality. I promote more programs and initiatives, but the life and teachings of Jesus, when embraced by any person who believes, can lift you up and bring you back! You need somebody that will shout, "Get up! You're not dead! Get up! I'm not finished with you! Get up! Get up! Get up! Get up!"

And one more thing to revive a child, you must have a concerned parent in the room, a sympathetic Savior that can call you back and a mind to make a comeback.

You need a mind to make a comeback. When Jesus called her, she came! She had a mind to make a comeback. She was only 12-years-old, and she had some type of feeling that this was not the end of her life. She knew that life was not over, so when He called, she came back. She got up at once. When daddy called her, she didn't come, that wasn't the right voice. When momma called her, she didn't come, that wasn't the right voice. When the mourners cried over her, she didn't come, that wasn't the right voice. When the people laughed at Jesus, she didn't come, that wasn't the right voice. But when Jesus called her, she got up!

Since she grew up in the church, she must have heard Luke 1:37, *"For nothing is impossible with God."* She must have heard Luke 2:49, *"Didn't you know, I must be about my fathers business."* She must have heard Luke 3:22, *"This is my beloved Son in whom I am well pleased."* She must have heard Luke 4:4, *"Man shall not live by bread alone but by every word that proceeds out of the mouth of God."* She must have heard Luke 5:31, *"I have not come to call the righteous but sinners to repentance."* She must have heard Luke 6:10, *"Stretch out your hand...and the hand was completely restored."* She must have heard Luke 7: 14, *"Young man, I say to you, get up!"*

The little girl was dead, and according to medical science, death is when signs of life in an organism cease. When a person's five senses have ceased, the person is considered dead. Here was a little girl, whose eyes were not open, so her sense of sight had ceased. She must be dead. She was not eating, so her sense of taste had ceased. She was not moving, so her sense of touch had ceased, she must be dead. She had no expression on her face from all the stink comments, so her sense of smell was gone. She must be dead. Four of her five senses had ceased, so she must be dead. But they must have overlooked her last remaining sense. Something happened that went past all systems and found a seat in her soul and it was the Word of God.

Not a message of mess. Not a flick of flesh. But she heard the Word from a man whom the book of Revelation describes as one riding a horse. Wearing a robe, dipped in blood, with a sword in hand and whose name is the Word of God! And when she heard Luke 8:54, "Talitha Cumi," which means, "my child, get up." She knew that God was talking to her and she had a mind to make a comeback. No matter what the situation, when He who was, and is, and is to come, calls you, you'd better be somewhere listening for your name.

When the resurrection and the life calls you back, you better have the mind to make a comeback. No matter how bad it looks, you can make a comeback. No matter how bad it gets, you can make a comeback. No matter how many times they break your heart, you can make a comeback. No matter how low your grades get, you can make a comeback. No matter how dead it looks, you can make a comeback. No matter how bad it smells, you can make a comeback. No matter how deep it is, you can make a comeback. No matter how bad you've been, you can make a comeback. Its revival time for the children!

I want to tell a little story about a young lady who was driving in the midst of a lightning storm. The woman's car had a sunroof and her little girl sat fastened securely in the back seat. Every time the lightning would flash, the little girl would look up at the lightning and smile. Her mother noticed her daughter do this several times, and when they arrived safely home, the woman asked her daughter, "I have a question for you. I don't understand how in the world you could smile in the midst of such a severe storm. We were riding through hell, through turmoil, through disappointment, through heartache and through pain! How in the world, could you just smile?"

She looked at her momma and said, "Momma, the reason I was smiling at the lighting was because God was taking my picture. He wanted to see how I looked in the midst of my storms!"

And right now, some of y'all are going through hell. Some of y'all are going through a bad situation, and God wants to know if you can praise Him in a dead situation. Can you dance when it gets real dirty? Can you clap when you can't see change? God wants to know, can you smile in the midst of a storm?

Jesus said, *"Suffer the little children to come unto me and forbid them not for such is the kingdom of heaven" (Matthew 19:14.)* Jesus said, *"I say unto you, 'Except ye be converted, and become as little children, ye shall not enter into the kingdom of heaven,'"* (Matthew 18:3). It's a child's revival! Find your guardian, find the sympathetic Savior, and make up your mind to make a comeback.

CHAPTER THREE

Are You Raising a Repeat Offender?

Focal Passage: 2nd Kings 17:29-41 (NRSV)

²⁹ But every nation still made gods of its own and put them in the shrines of the high places that the people of Samaria had made, every nation in the cities in which they lived; ³⁰the people of Babylon made Succoth-benoth, the people of Cuth made Nergal, the people of Hamath made Ashima; ³¹the Avvites made Nibhaz and Tartak; the Sepharvites burned their children in the fire to Adrammelech and Anammelech, the gods of Sepharvaim. ³²They also worshipped the LORD and appointed from among themselves all sorts of people as priests of the high places, who sacrificed for them in the shrines of the high places. ³³So they worshipped the LORD, but they also served their own gods, after the manner of the nations from among whom they had been carried away. ³⁴To this day they continue to practice their former customs.

They do not worship the Lord and they do not follow the statutes or the ordinances or the law or the commandment that the Lord commanded the children of Jacob, whom he named Israel. ³⁵The Lord had made a covenant with them and commanded them, 'You shall not worship other gods or bow yourselves to them or serve them or sacrifice to them, ³⁶but you shall worship the Lord, who brought you out of the land of Egypt with great power and with an outstretched arm; you shall bow yourselves to him, and to him you shall sacrifice. ³⁷The statutes and the ordinances and the law and the commandment that he wrote for you, you shall always be careful to observe. You shall not worship other gods; ³⁸you shall not forget the covenant that I have made with you. You shall not worship other gods, ³⁹but you shall worship the Lord your God; he will deliver you out of the hand of all your enemies.' ⁴⁰They would not listen, however, but they continued to practice their former custom. ⁴¹ So these nations worshipped the Lord, but also served their carved images; to this day their children and their children's children continue to do as their ancestors did.

There was a little boy that lived in a house that had a cookie jar in the kitchen, on the counter near the fridge. And in order to enjoy the crispy, crunchy cookies, the rule was to ask for permission. Well, the little boy did not see a need to ask for permission since the person who brought the cookies, brought them for everybody's enjoyment. So the little boy would sneak into the kitchen and eat the cookies from the cookie jar, one at a time not thinking that any one would notice, because everybody in the house loved the cookies in the cookie jar.

One day, while strategizing how to get a cookie from the cookie jar, he got caught and was reminded that the policy was to ask for permission to get cookies from the cookie jar. The little boy was found guilty of taking cookies from the jar and told not to do it again. But as soon as he was alone in the house, he went right back to that cookie jar, got a cookie and went back to the couch. When his parents got home, they asked him, "Did you eat cookies from the cookie jar?" And he said, "No." Then they said, "Well, who left this trail of crumbs to the couch?" He was caught again and the parents understood that they were dealing with a repeat offender.

Now a cookie from the cookie jar might be something small to you, but what happens when a cookie turns into a crayon? What happens when the crayon turns into a car? What happens when a car turns into an entire community? What happens when the child or person repeats the crime again and again? And offends again and again? What happens when the person breaks law after law? Caught and found guilty. And for some reason it is not a new crime. What do you do when someone does the same thing over and over again? It can be functionally identical, appropriately indistinguishable, just alike, impossible to tell apart, yet one and the same. It can be equivalent to a prior offense. What happens when it is the same thing you did last time, and the time before that. What do you do with a repeat offender?

Someone who has become habitual in causing you displeasure, customary in causing confusion and consistent in causing chaos? How do you deal with someone who violates vicariously, resents regularly, angers reliably and wounds whole-heartedly? Nobody likes to deal with a repeat offender. If they did it once, we can understand. But if they do it again, somebody ought to lock them up and throw away the key. They ought to go to jail, and straight to jail. Do no pass go and do not collect 200 dollars. What do you do with a repeat offender?

Here we are in Israel, 400 years of slavery and you come out with a free trip through the Red Sea. 40 years of repeat offenses and some of your children still made it to the Promise Land. You turned your back and served Balaam (*ruin*), and He still gave you judges to deliver you from the hand of your enemies. When your sons (Eli) served Belial, He still raised up Samuel as a priest in His stead. When you cried out for a king and not the King of Kings, He gave you Saul. When you were in sorrow, He gave you a song in David. But you kept on doing your thing.

In the book of Kings, we find the details of the stages God's people go through under certain kings. The nations are split because of their disobedience and amnesia. And for 22 years, they suffer the junk of Jeroboam (*the people increased*). And for two years, the nothingness of Nadab (*liberal or present spontaneously*). And for 24 years of the bum-fuddles of Baasha (to stink, offensiveness). And for two years, the inebriation of Elah (*an oak or other strong tree*). And for seven days, the improprieties of Zimri (*musical*). They suffer the 12 years of oversights of Omir (*heaping*). And the 22 years of artfuls of Ahab (*father's brother*). And the two years of arrest of Ahaziah (*God sustains*). The 12 years of junk from Jehu (*Jehovah (is) He*), Jehoahaz (*Jehovah-Seized*), Jehoash (*Jehovah-fired*) and Jeroaboam. Then on to the zeal of Zechariah (*God has remembered*), the solecism of Shallum (*shorter*), the misconceptions of Menaham (*comforter*), the problems of Pekahiah (*watch*), the pratfall of Pekah (*watch*) and here in 2nd Kings with horrible Hoshea (*deliverer*). God decides to bring them out one more time in a massive resettlement project and instead of praising only the true and living God, they decide to bring their own gods with them, bowing down to the false images of the real thing.

And the text records that they worship the Lord and serve their own national gods. Brought out by the real thing, yet they still return to serve that which cannot save and protect. They did it before and they are doing it again. And we want to call them repeat offenders. But our focus today is that not only were they doing it then, but some still do it today. They worship the Lord and serve their gods and teach their children to do it and their children's children. These offenses are functionally identical and equivalent to a prior offense. They are repeat offenders just like their fathers, and their father's father. But what if you are raising a repeat offender?

How do you know if you are raising a repeat offender?

[29] But every nation still made gods of its own and put them in the shrines of the high places that the people of Samaria had made, every nation in the cities in which they lived;

What are you making them bow down to or look up to?

In our text, we find these nationalities are making gods of their own. And placing those gods in high places, known as the place where they would inquire of their god with a sacrifice. We find a group of people erecting a representation or carved image of a god and placing it in a place where it can interact with its worshippers. And they sacrifice to it, for inquiry. We find a group of humans manufacturing a substitute for the true and living God, reverencing it and even making sacrifices for it to provide a false message. And they bow down to it and they look up to it to worship and adore.

What false image are we making our children bow down to? Are we making them bow down to the dried up American dream? Are we making them bow down to time alone so that we can work to be like somebody else? Are we making them bow down to low-riders and rims? What false message are we upholding in front of them? Do as I say and not as I do? Who are we making them look up to, P-Diddy, Lil Wayne or Charles

Barkley? Where is the Martin King in their life, non-violent resistance? Where is the Madame C.J. Walker in their life, the entrepreneur? Where is the Harriet Tubman, the freedom rider? Where is the big momma, the wisdom giver? Where is the Uncle Willie, the revolutionary? Where is the Barack Obama, the call for change? What are we making them become vulnerable too? Who are we making them open up too? How do we know if we are raising a repeat offender? Look at what we are making them bow down to and look up to.

Secondary Verse 30 says, *³⁰the people of Babylon made Succoth-benoth, the people of Cuth made Nergal, the people of Hamath made Ashima; ³¹the Avvites made Nibhaz and Tartak; the Sepharvites burned their children in the fire to Adrammelech and Anammelech, the gods of Sepharvaim.*

What are you making them walk through?

In our text, the represented nationalities worshipped many gods. They wanted to please their gods. But in order to please one of the gods named, Molech, they had to offer a child sacrifice. A child was either thrown into the fire or made to walk through the fire and be consumed.

What are you making your child walk through? Some of us wake up and throw our children into the hands of MTV, BET and VH1. Some of us wake up and throw our children into the hands of unsafe child care providers. Some of us wake up and throw our children into the hands of gang members. Some of us wake up and throw our children into under-funded schools and never make time to get involved with the PTA, and never make time to march to city hall to make changes. What are you making your child walk through?

There are moms who didn't win beauty pageants as little girls and now they dress their own daughters as doll babies to satisfy their own ambitions. There are fathers making their sons become football, basketball and baseball players to fulfill one of their deferred dreams. There are moms dressing their 3-year-old sons like thugs so that they can look like the gangster that they never found. There are fathers playing rough with their baby boys so that they will learn to resist pain and learn aggression to avoid getting pushed around in elementary school.

In our text, these nations continued to worship the Lord, yet they served their own gods. They even appointed priests to minister in their place. The same thing that caused them to be carried away in the beginning is the same thing they did when they returned to Samaria. How in the world do we find the energy to return to the same thing that got us in trouble in the first place? Here we are worshipping the Lord yet serving our own gods. Here we are falling down before the Lord, yet standing up on the god of our own making. Here we are bowing down before the Lord, yet waiting on our own god. Here we are respecting the Lord, yet banking on the reputation of our own god. Here we are sanctifying the Lord, yet satisfying our own god. Here we are praising the Lord, yet promoting our own god. Here we are blessing the Lord, yet benefiting from our own god. Here we are honoring the Lord, yet sometimes ministering to our own god.

How in the world did they trick themselves into worshipping the Lord and serving their own gods?

We were in trouble before and here we are again. It offended God. It violated Him. It displeased Him. It abused Him. It shocked Him. It provoked Him. It wounded Him. But now our children are doing the same thing.

God says, "I am the Lord. You shall not worship any other, bow down to, or sacrifice to any other god but Me! Don't you remember? I brought you out of Egypt, under Pharaoh's rule. Don't you remember? I held you up when you were weak. Don't you remember? Your enemies drowned in the Red Sea. Don't you remember? I held you up in the wilderness, led you with a pillar of cloud by day and a pillar of fire by night. Don't you remember? I gave you manna from heaven and fed you until you wanted no more. All you had to do is remember to keep my commands. And the first one is thou shall have no other God before me. Remember the covenant I made with you?" And the thing that God wants you to remember is the same thing you want them to remember about you.

Verse 38 says,

38you shall not forget the covenant that I have made with you. You shall not worship other gods, 39but you shall worship the LORD your God; he will deliver you out of the hand of all your enemies.'

Finally, if you want to know if you are raising a repeat offender, ask yourself, "What do you want them to remember from you?"

I've realized that this millennial generation is non-verbal and visual. They don't do what you tell them from the heart, they do what you show them from the heart. They have the ability is emulate the lifestyle, characteristics and behavior of the people they see. Do as I say, not as I do, doesn't work with them. What do you want them to remember from you? When was the last time they saw you praying? And I'm not talking about the Lord's Prayer, "Our father, which art in heaven." But a prayer that came from the recesses of your soul, "Father, I stretch my hand to thee."

When was the last time they saw you praising God? Not the patty-cake praise, but a praise that got on your neighbors nerves. When was the last time they saw you repent? Not just, "Lord, I'm sorry," but the one that says, "Create in me a clean heart and renew the right spirit in me." When was the last time they saw you dancing before the Lord? Not just a surface dance, but an undignified praise. When was the last time they saw you feed the homeless? Not just when its convenient like holidays and special media occasions, but when you have to stop your car on the side of the road to give somebody a biscuit and barbecue dinner. When was the last time they saw you forgive your enemies? Not just to say it, but to go a step further and take your enemy out to lunch. When was the last time they saw you kiss your wife? Not just a peck, but a throw your arms around her and caress her so gently that she melts in your arms kind of kiss. When was the last time they saw you build up your man in his weakest hour? Not just to leave him to himself, but to cut-back on expenses when times were tough and take one-pound of ground beef and make it feed the whole family.

When was the last time you got lost in God's presence while you were driving the car? Not to just keep driving, but to actually pull over and give God some praise for the door He just opened, and to thank Him for being an awesome God and a strong-tower.

What you want them to remember will determine if they become a repeat offender. The Lord said, "I want you to remember my covenant, and the condition is this: You cannot worship idol gods, but worship only the Lord God." He will deliver you out of the hands of all of your enemies. If you remember the agreement, you will receive the achievement. If you remember the bond, you will receive the breakthrough. If you remember the condition, you will receive the connection. The deal is connected to the deliverance. The promise is connected to the promotion. The testament is connected to the testimony. Make sure you don't forget that God will deliver you from all of your enemies. The weapons may form but they will not prosper. In other words, if you remember God's covenant,

He will give you breakout power from all of your enemies.

God will give you slip-away power. They may try to grab you, but you, like David will remember, "He has anointed my head with oil, and my cup runneth over." The oil is a slippery substance that gives you slip-away power.

God will give you cactus power. A cactus has spikes on its outer shell to protect it from external invaders. He will give you cactus power to keep external forces from taking you over and taking you out. Nobody in their right mind bothers a cactus. If you remember His promise, He will give you the power to withstand any obstacle.

God will give you spider power. A spider has the ability to never get caught in its own web. He will give you spider power so that when internal conflicts come out of you or against you, your body, like the spider, will produce oil so that you never get caught in the web you created. If you remember His covenant, He will give you power to overcome internal conflicts.

Remember the Lord, He is God. He is a rock in a weary land! Don't serve them, serve Him! He is the real thing! He is the answer! He will never let you down! He will never leave you alone! And even after all of this, the text says, "They would not listen." They continued in their former ways. They kept doing what they'd always done. As it turned out, all the time these people were putting on a front of worshipping God, they were at the same time involved with their local idols. And they're still doing it, like father, like son.

Are you raising a repeat offender? What are you making them look up to? What are you making them walk through? What do you want them to remember about you? If you obey His commands, He will deliver you and you will save the next generation!

CHAPTER FOUR

How to Secure Our Future: Look at What You Have in Hand

Focal Passage: Psalm 127:1-5 (NIV)

¹ Unless the LORD builds the house, its builders labor in vain. Unless the LORD watches over the city, the watchmen stand guard in vain. ² In vain you rise early and stay up late, toiling for food to eat—for he grants sleep to [a] those he loves. ³ Sons are a heritage from the LORD, children a reward from him. ⁴ Like arrows in the hands of a warrior are sons born in one's youth. ⁵ Blessed is the man whose quiver is full of them. They will not be put to shame when they contend with their enemies in the gate.

Have you noticed how much time people spend in futile endeavors? Have you noticed how much time people invest in completing tasks that are incapable of producing any result? Maybe this doesn't apply to you, but do you know somebody that is just busy but unproductive? A person with a full plate but is never able to eat it all? Someone who has many fish to fry, but is never able to taste one bite? Do you know someone with so many irons in the fire, they are constantly hustling, in a meeting, in a conference, in someone else's possession, in the field or in the laboratory and yet they are never able to produce anything from it?

What about people who just like to look busy? They beat their heads against the wall, can't focus on anything. Just busy, so busy in life they can't even stay awake when they come to church. Do you know people that are just busy but are never able to do any business?

What about us? What are we busy doing? Are we busy doing things that don't matter? Are we having conversations that don't matter? Are we fighting over things that don't even matter? Are we holding grudges that don't even matter? Are we missing out on a life of rest, mercy and favor because we are too busy? The post-modern culture that we live in has a way of keeping us busy. We keep chasing after a dream that has cost the lives of so many of our ancestors. If we just have to be busy, I want to ask what are we busy doing? ·

Are we busy in the school system, confronting the issues of why the majority of minority public school districts receive nearly 1,000 dollars less per student than other majority school districts, or are we just busy trying to make a point in Sunday school? Are we busy trying to confront issues of why only 52% of minorities have no health insurance and 30% of those 52% sit in church every Sunday, or are we trying to decide what hat to wear? Are we busy trying to decrease the number of African Americans living below the poverty line? Or trying to decrease the 50% HIV/AIDS rate found among African Americans, of which 69% affected are African American women?

Did you know that once arrested, minorities are three times more likely than majorities to be incarcerated again? And we are hurting people's feelings, forgetting our faith, neglecting our calls and denying our children, all for the sake to say we are busy. Are we so busy building a house that we can't see that what we have in the house is tearing it down from the inside out? Some of us are so busy out there in life, grabbing for everything that comes our way. We have to do everything, have to be everywhere, and have to go with everybody. Rising early, staying out late, toiling and toiling, trying to beat the next man.

Something must be done, but not everything. Sometimes we have to sit down and rest. Unless the Lord builds a house, they that labor do it in vain? Unless the Lord keeps the city, they that watch do it in vain. We can spend all of our energy doing things, controlling things, worrying over things, crying over things, walking over things on the floor. But look to the hills from whence cometh our help. Know our help comes from the Lord, who is the maker of heaven and earth. He will not suffer thy foot to be moved, the Lord who keeps thee. He will not slumber nor sleep. If the Lord is awake, why are we pacing the floor? Sit down somewhere and rise up to do that which will produce a useful result.

The Lord is thy keeper; the Lord is thy shade upon thy right. The sun shall not smite thee by day, nor the moon by night, He shall preserve thy soul. If gospel artist, Rev. Charles Nicks, was here, he would say, "All of my help comes from the Lord." If we are working with the Lord, He will give us rest; and not just eternal rest, but some rest right here on earth. In an effort to capture the sometimes restless and yet hopeful emotions and attitudes of the people of God over a 500 year period, writers wrote songs of sorrow and joy, despair and hope, doubt and trust, pain and consolation and anger and contentment.

They would sing songs that went like Thomas Dorsey's original piece, "When my way grows dear precious Lord linger near, when my life is almost got, hear my cry, hear my call, hold my hand lest I fall," songs of sorrow. But yet they sang songs of joy that ask in the words of Rev. Clay Evans, "Have You Got Good Religion," and the response would be "Certainly Lord." They sang songs of doubt, like in the words of Brenda Waters, "I don't know how God's gonna do, I don't know when, He's gonna fix it." But they followed with a song of faith in the words of Rev. James Moore, "Then I said to my soul, soul take courage, the Lord will make a way somehow."

These songs and our focal text in particular answered

the emotional needs of the people of God while they were on their way to the temple. The writers had a way of capturing the real experiences of people and setting it to a tune that would be beneficial for generations to come. They knew there would be a group of people who would be faced with the challenges of business, ineffectiveness, success and trivial living. But the unique thing about Psalms is that they used their experience to express their condition and also God's provision.

One of our favorite Psalmist's illustrates this when he said, "Thou preparest a table before me in the presence of mine enemies, and yet thou has anointed my head with oil and my cup runneth." It speaks to their condition but it also speaks to God's provision.

We also note the Psalmist saying, "When my enemies come in like a flood, the spirit of the Lord shall lift us a standard against, though a host encamp around yet in this will I be comforted." It speaks to our condition, yet it speaks to God's provision. When you are a child of God, don't ever think of your condition without considering God's provision.

In our focal passage, God's provision helps us to understand how God plans to secure our future: It is God's 401-K plan. It is God's way of setting us up for an expected end. It is God's agreement of assurance. It is God's contract of coverage. It is God's guarantee of good things. It is God's promise of provision. It is God's redemption of restitution. It is how God intends for every system, for every dispensation, for every house, home, building, city, people and pride to secure their future. And the Psalmist reveals to us that it is our children. God's plan to protect us, save us and preserve us is right in our children.

We may want something outside of us to bless us, we may want the thing that we worked for to protect us, but God's system of salvation is in our sons. God's deal of deliverance is in our daughters. And the Bible says the periscope of the morning is a gift. It does not matter what circumstances brought them here, if they made it, they are a gift. Not a grudge, but they are a gift. They are not a burden, they are a blessing. They are not excess baggage, they are an endowment. They are not a task, they are a token. The Bible in our text calls them a heritage from the Lord. I understand that sometimes they act like the seed of Chuckie, but they are a gift from the Lord. So I ask the question, have you neglected the gift of the Lord?

When God gave us children, God did us a favor, out of His goodwill. God did it just because God likes us and it was a favor. Oh don't act like you ain't never had a favor. You didn't deserve it, you didn't earn it, God just did it and God doesn't want anything back; it was His favor to you. The Psalmist tells us in verse 3, that children are a blessing and a gift from the Lord. Like arrows in the hand of a mighty warrior are the son's of one's youth. I want to suggest a few things to those potential borderline busybodies who are depending on their work, strength and influence alone to secure their future in these uncertain times to look at what you have in hand.

May I suggest that what you have in hand came from the Lord as a reward to you. Children are a gift from God to provide security for parents, guardians, mentors and leaders. If you are ever in a place where there are no children, run because there is nothing there to keep you alive. Children are a sign that God's favor is on the house. If people were able to be in contact with children, it is because God was trying to give them hope for their future. And not just children that came from your womb, but children who you have the opportunity to impact, and influence that are not biologically your own. They are a gift. You didn't earn the opportunity to bless a child; you were given the opportunity to bless a child.

And if you are trying to look to your future security, look at what you have in hand. Moses had a rod in his hand. David had a slingshot and five smooth stones. The widow had just enough left to bake a cake and die. The indebted woman had one jar of oil that kept flowing. Everything these folks needed to make sure they stayed alive was right in their hands. I encourage you to look at what you have in hand.

Because what you have right now, if you have handled it carefully and have given it over to God, it will assure you that God is on the house. They are a gift and reward to you. Who else can lead like you? Your children. Who else can love like you? Your children. Who else can teach like you? Your children. Who else can pick up where you left off? Your children. Who else can go farther than you imagined? Your children. And they are a gift to you. You ought to thank God for your gift. Stop complaining to people about your gift. Stop pushing your gift off on somebody else. Stop letting somebody else cultivate your gift. Stop letting drug dealers, gangbangers, Rihanna, Trey Songz, Barney, Dora the Explorer, Hannah Montana and Lil Wayne have more influence on your gift than you have.

Beyonce ain't got nothing on you. Drake ain't got nothing on you. Snoop Dogg ain't got nothing on you. And you may not think it, but the kids they hang around with ain't got nothing on that which the Lord have given you charge over. You ought to begin to stop crying about your gift and begin to praise God for your gift and if the gift is pointed in the wrong direction, praise God until He turns the gift He gave you around. Stop complaining about the gifts God gave you. Thank God for your gift.

Secondly, I want to suggest from the phrase "like arrows in the hands of warriors, so are children of ones youth," that what you have in your hand will define who you are.

Warriors are said to have arrows, parents are said to have children, so what is in your hands? Arrows rest in the hands of warriors and children rest in the hands of parents. Which are you? What you have in your hand will tell us who you are. Or have you dropped your arrows and let go of your children? Have you come to battle without any weapons to fight or have you gotten so frustrated that you have turned your children over to the system to survive on their own? Were you running so fast to get to the battle that you lost your arrows or are you so tired after you get from work that you allow BET and MTV to teach your child about life? Have you been so busy buying their friendship that you forgot to be a parent? Have you been so intentional in trying to not raise them like your parents raised you that they can't even distinguish your voice when you call them by their names?

Have you been so angry with the parent that did not stay, that you distorted their vision of what parenting is all about? Have you been so busy trying to make them be what your partner was not that they have a hard time distinguishing which direction they will go in relational expression? Have you been so busy letting them lead you instead of training them in the way that they should go? What you have in your hand will define who you are.

Are you a warrior or a weakling? Are you a father or a fan? Are you a mother or a mischief-maker? Are you an encourager or an evil-doer? Are you a warrior or a wretch? Are you a matriarch or a miscreant? Are you a provider or a performer? What do you have in your Hand? Because what you have in your hand defines who you are. Can you still reach out and grab your child? Or have they gotten so far away from you that your arms can't reach? Whose hands are they in? Whose voice do they hear? Whose words do they remember? And whose cause do they carry? Because what you have in your hand will define who you are.

The question is who are you? Are you a warrior or have you come to the battle unprepared? The fifth verse of this expression of God's provision for their condition, and this psalm of praise are a reason for going to the temple and lifting up the Lord, who says, "Happy is the man whose quiver if full of them." The text says the more you have the better off you will be, because they will protect you when your enemies attack you in the gates and in some translations the courts.

Thirdly, I want to suggest to those who want to have a grip on the future in the midst of uncertain times to look at what you have in hand. Not only because what you have in hand is a reward and gift to you from the Lord, not only does it define who you are, but lastly that *what you have in hand will protect you in places of vulnerability.*

In the text, the most vulnerable place for the family of God was at the gates of the city. At the gates of the city were the rulers and courts. It was the place where you would have to go and defend your cause in public. It was the place where they decided if what you have been busy doing was worth anything. It was where they decided if your life's work was of any value. It was where the people decided if your concern was valid or not. It was where they decided if you were a force to be reckoned with or someone who needed to be overtaken because you had nothing to show for all of your toil and labor in the field and in their lives.

It was in this place where the old folks would say: may

the work I've done speak for me. But here in the text, when the father shows up with a multitude of sons, it let the public know that this father had done what God had required him to do and he would be protected. When you show up to the court with sons, let the powers that be, know that they are not your source and supply, but that God has given you children who will look after you even in your old age. When they show up with you, let the powers know that your name is not dead because you have an heir to carry on the family name and legacy.

Thank God for what you have in your hand. For what you have in your hand will protect you in the moment of attack. Oh don't worry; you will get to your moment of attack. You will have some enemies in the gate. The text speaks to those who have gotten to full maturity, and full maturity has a level of enemies of its own. You don't have to look far; you who have matured have some enemies that you know very well. You used to have 20/20 vision, but there is an enemy that causes your eyes to draw dim. You used to have a full head of hair, but there is an enemy that has chased the hair clean off of your head. And if you have some hair left, there is an enemy that causes that remaining hair to change to either gray or white.

We used to have 32 teeth, but there is an enemy that has changed those incisors, canines, molars and premolars into implants, partials, bridges and dentures. Oh you can act like you don't know what I'm talking about; we have some enemies in the gate. And if you don't have them right now, you just live a little longer and you will find out that just living life has its enemies. You can run now, but one day your steps will get shorter and your pace will slow down. You can sleep all you want now, but one day you will find yourself barely sleeping at all.

Bone density will weaken, muscles will get weaker, it is an enemy of life and one day everybody meets it. And when these days come, your children will be there to help you make it through.

But this is the promise, if you look at what you have in hand; God will use what you have in hand to rise up and protect you and provide for you in your old age.

If you want a little security, you better be careful how you handle what you have in hand. Because what you have is God's plan for provision for your church, your home, your life and your ministry.

Sons are a gift from God. Now I understand why the people were shouting, Hosanna to the Son of David! Blessed is He who comes in the name of the Lord, as Jesus was making His triumphant entry into Jerusalem, they recognized that He was the Son of God, and since He was the Son of God, He was on the scene to protect the people of God. If Jesus is here, it tells us that God is not dead, but He is alive and well.

The Son keeps the name alive. The Son continues the legacy. The Son takes us farther. The Son lifts us up. The Son brings us out. The Son leads us through. The Son leads us in. The Son fights for us. The Son dies for us. The Son recovers us.

The Son restores us. Thank God for the Son. Sons are a reward from the Lord. The Son rises for us. The Son returns for us. The Son picks us up and carries us on to meet the Father.

Look at what you have in hand. I am reminded in Genesis 33, when Jacob and Esau were about to reconcile, that Jacob, whose name means supplanter and trickster, was about to reconcile with his brother, Esau, whose name means hunter and hairy. Esau, who remembered that he had been tricked before, I suggest must have remembered the slickness of his brother. And you know how it is when you are going back home for the first time, everybody is going to be looking at you to see what you are made of yourself after you messed up real bad. It was his moment of truth and validation. And the Bible said, Jacob looked up and saw Esau coming, he had 400 men with him. Esau ran ahead to meet his brother, and Jacob asked who all those people were. And Esau replied, "These are the children that God has blessed me with."

That is why I encourage you to look at what you have in hand, because what you have may one day have to protect you from you own kinfolk. The children are a blessing from the Lord, they define who you are and they will rise up to meet with your enemies in the gate. If you want to secure your future, you have to use what you have in hand.

Even God, used what He had in hand. He thought to Himself, and said my birthday is coming, and I'm gonna turn from the young age of time to the old age of eternity, and I need to secure my future. And being not only a God of grace and mercy, but also a God of war, He looked around the kingdom of heaven, and reviewed His possessions. God remembered that He had a quiver on His back, one called Son and the other called Holy Ghost. If there was anybody who would secure the family name, if there was one that would take care of the kingdom, it could only be the Son.

Keeping in the culture, the Son became an arrow shot out of heaven with the bow of God. God aimed the arrow for one place. When the point of engagement was secure, God shot the arrow called Son. The arrow went down through 42 generations, but that was not the destination. The arrow went through the baptism waters of John, but that was not the destination. The arrow healed the blind, and raised the dead, but that was not the destination. Remember every true warrior hits it target because he shoots with the mind that he may only have one chance. The arrow went through a garden called Gethsemane, but that was not its destination. The arrow flew past Pilate, and curved around Herod, but that was not its destination. The arrow survived the winds of whipping, the arrow survived the words of taunting and the arrow survived the tears of tyranny because that was not its destination.

But when the arrow hit the cross, it had met the intended point of impact. When the arrow hit the cross, it had hit its target of intention. When the arrow hit the cross, it proved that there was a real warrior at its origination, for He was the Lamb slain from the foundation of the earth. When the arrow hit the wood and the blood came streaming down. It washed every sin from the beginning of time to the present day. The blood cleansed every emotion of hatred and jealousy. The blood was so powerful that it reached to the highest mountain and flowed to the lowest valley. The blood was the sign of a successful impact. God used what He had in hand to secure His future.

CHAPTER FIVE

I Just Wanna Be Successful

Focal Passage: Joshua 1:7-8

⁷ Only be thou strong and very courageous, that thou mayest observe to do according to all the law, which Moses my servant commanded thee: turn not from it to the right hand or to the left, that thou mayest prosper withersoever thou goest. ⁸ This book of the law shall not depart out of thy mouth; but thou shalt meditate therein day and night, that thou mayest observe to do according to all that is written therein: for then thou shalt make thy way prosperous, and then thou shalt have good success.

The title of this message is not my own. It comes from the chorus of a song by Hip Hop artist, Drake that features Trey Songz and rapper Lil Wayne, entitled, "Successful." It has been raised out of concern that this message is misleading our young people as it relates to the measure of success. In the lyrics of this song, success has been chopped up and reduced to the acquisition of money, cars, clothes, and hoes as if having this is what makes one successful.

The measure of success for these brothers is the ability to acquire the money. The money leads way to the cars. And if you have a nice car, you're gonna need some nice clothes to wear while you are riding around in the car. Now the cars are not owned but leased. And lastly, the cars and the clothes lead to females who throw themselves at brothers who own nothing, call them out of their names, think their thoughts are worth nickels and spend thousands of dollars on drinks and parties. Their plans for the future are bleak and almost non-existent.

What a message. As of January 2014 the song has been viewed 17,370,204 times on YouTube. In 2011 it played on BET everyday. And it can be heard on radio stations across this nation up to 4 times per day. Some people have the chorus downloaded as a ringtone on their phones. And it is not just young people. Some old folks just want the money, the money and the cars, the cars and the clothes and the clothes and the hoes. They just want to be successful.

Success measured like this only leads to unchallenged and uncritical pursuits. These pursuits don't cause us to advance. Some bring us right back into the mess and condition we were in from the beginning, stuck between a rock and a hard place because of the unchallenged decisions in our pursuit of success.

This sounds like a great place to identify a group who are also stuck. The Bible records how the children of God were stuck between the plains of Moab and the Jordan River. Stuck between where they have been settled and where God had called them to go. Have you ever been stuck with what you settled for and saw the promise right beyond the river but could not get there? Stuck in a job that will not ever promote you to a place where all your gifts can be used. Sometimes people are not stuck; they are just comfortable with where they are. They know there is more out there, but they refuse to step out and go after the more.

They would rather settle on this when they have access to that. They would rather do just enough, even though they have the potential to be the best. They would rather take the shortcut instead of the road that would lead them to a confident destination. They are stuck, I mean comfortable.

Here are God's people, right around the plains where the land is low and the view is clear, a place where the hills are low and if the enemy would come up against them they would have time to get ready to fight. It was where they were comfortable but it was not where they were called.

But these were God's people, and whenever God's people get stuck, God is obligated to raise up somebody that will lead His people from the place of boredom to the place called blessing. Somebody that will lead them across the muddy waters of the Jordan so they can reach their promise. In our text, God commissions Joshua to lead the people and the first thing God wants to talk to this young new leader about, are the Keys to Success. Not Drake's success, but real success, real triumph and real achievement. To the Joshua's of this generation, let me talk to you about how to get a real breakthrough to obtain real happiness and to have victory in all your battles. In verse 7, God instructs Joshua to, *"turn not to the right, or the left, that thou mayest prosper whithersover thou goest."*

Joshua's mini lesson on the secrets to success, calls for him to concentrate.

The American College Dictionary defines *concentrate* as "the ability to direct one's thoughts or attention." If we want to be successful, we have to learn how to concentrate. We have to focus our efforts and our energies. We have to concentrate. We have to devote ourselves to what it is that we are doing. Some of us are just unfocused; trying to do it all and we find ourselves coming up short every time. Some of us are trying to be a student, a parent, a counselor, a brother and a friend. Some of us are trying to do everything under the sun. Sit down somewhere and concentrate. Focus your efforts and do that one thing well.

You don't have to be in the pulpit, in the choir, at the door, in the kitchen or running the meeting. Concentrate. You don't have to be on the phone, killing the cow, taking out the trash and fussing, sit down and get focused. You don't have to have your hand in the cookie jar, the candy jar and the doughnut rack all at the same time, sit down and concentrate. You don't have to balance a honey through text, a pie through email, a good one through Gmail and another one on AOL, concentrate.

We have to learn how to concentrate because the more things we attempt to do, the more diluted we become. Meaning that what we do gets less and less of us every time we pour into it. Don't try to do everything, just do that one thing you are committed to. Lutheran Theologian, Frederich Keil says it like this:

"As the soldier of an earthly leader is to act in all things according to certain rules laid down in a code drawn up for the purpose, so the Christian soldier has his code drawn up for him by God Himself, and revealed to him in the oracles of truth. This code, he is to study with diligence, that he may conform himself to it in every particular. This will require all the courage any man can possess."

God speaks to Joshua and says, "If you want to be successful, concentrate, devote yourself and your efforts to what you are doing." Concentrate.

Secondly, God instructs this new leader at the time of great transition that success comes from meditation. In verse 8, God instructs Joshua to meditate. The Buddhists and the Hindus define *meditation* as the "act of training, calming or emptying the mind as focusing on a single object." But that's not the meditation God is talking about to Joshua. God is instructing Joshua to reflect on and contemplate in a deliberative manner on the words I have spoken to you. If you are going to be successful Joshua, you must come to the place where you never let what I have said be away from your mind. God wants Joshua to have His word and His agenda in mind at all times.

We have to meditate; the Hebrew word for *meditate* here is "hagah (haw-gaw)" which means, "to ponder: imagine, mourn, mutter, to roar, to talk, study and utter." I want to use the portion of the meaning that says, to meditate is to roar. When lions roar, it is a loud sound from within that signals other lions that the lion is present. God tells Joshua, you are going to hear many things, you are going to fight many battles, you will hear many strategies and you will hear many methods. But when you hear them, I need what I say to you to be set on the volume of roar in you so that you will be able to do what I have told you and I will lead you to success. I need you to let healing roar on the inside when they say sickness from the outside. I need you to hear deliverance roaring on the inside when they say you will never come out from the outside. I need you to meditate and let what I have said to you roar in you at all times. And what I say is roaring to let the adversary know, I'm in here, and you better think twice before you come messing with me. You have to learn how to meditate.

Thirdly, Joshua, if you want to be successful, you must do some observation. Concentration is good, meditation is even better but observation is the main key. This understanding of observation is not the one where you just look at what I said, because there are some that just look at my word. This understanding is not a looking, it is a doing. If you want to be successful you have to do something.

The definition of *observation* here is to "act in conformity with heed, live by and obey God's Word." Joshua, do not just hear my voice but act in conformity with what I say.

Your life has to be a pattern of the Word of God spoken to you. Joshua, if you want to be successful you have to heed, live by and obey my Word. So many times we want to hear it, but we don't want to do it. But if you want the success of God on your life, you must bring your life into alignment with the Word of God. We must not be hearers only but doers also. We must do the Word of God. I know some of us have it all figured out from the wisdom of man, but we have to go back to doing the Word of God:

I⁻ *Peter 1:6 says, "Be ye Holy, for I am Holy."* We've go to do the Word.

II Corinthians 2:10 says, "Forgive anything, and I will forgive you also."

We've got to do the Word. Every person in the Bible who has ever been successful had to do the Word of God. He told Samson not to touch the vineyard. He told David not to walk in the council of the ungodly. He told Moses and Joshua to take off their shoes for the Ground they stand on is Holy. They had to do the Word. Don't just hear it, but take it to the next level and do it. Do what II Corinthians (6:17) says, *"Come out from among them and be ye separate.*" Do what I Thessalonians (5:17) says, "*Pray without ceasing.*" Do what Ephesians 5:25 says, "*Love your wife as Jesus loved the church.*" Do what Exodus 20:12 says, "*Honor your mother and father, that your days may be long upon the land.*" Do what Psalms 150 says and "*praise Him with the timbrel and dance*". Do what Psalms 100 says and "*make a joyful noise unto the Lord all ye lands.*"

Rev. F.G. Marchant puts it like this:

"*He who walks with the Bible may sing with Paul, 'All things work together for the good to them that love God, to them who are called according to his purposes.'*"

You have to do the Word. Don't just look at it, look to do it. Joshua, if you are going to have success you have to do the Word.

Lastly, one more thing: success comes with concentration, meditation and observation. But God promises Joshua more than success, He promises him good success. All successes aren't considered good. If you want good success, you have to have the right associations. In verse 5 and 9, there is a phrase of text that stands out as a key to good success. It is the statement that says: "*I am with thee*" and "*the Lord You God is with thee.*"

Rev. F.G. Marchant says:

"*The Word of God is the mind of God, and he who keeps ever with the law is always where God stoops to whisper, 'I am with thee.'*"

If you want to have good success you have got to have the

right associations. *Association* is defined as "connections and links between two or more persons or bodies." Association is synonymous with the words accompanying, alongside, among, beside or near. Some of us just have the wrong associations. We have the wrong common interests and have formed the wrong type of link to one or more bodies. Many of us want to be more, but we keep having common interests with less. Many of us want to be better, but we keep company with those who don't want to get better. Many of us want to get up, but we stay linked with those who are determined to stay down. We want a better marriage, but we have common interests with those who destroy marriages. We want a better life, but we keep hanging with those who are content to stay right where they are in the slums. We may have the wrong people, mindsets or laws running alongside us and that may be keeping us from the good success that God has given to us.

But Joshua, if you want good success, you have to have the Lord God Almighty with you. The Lord says to Joshua while Joshua is by himself, "*I am with you.*"

Richard Nelson comments:

"Yahweh's pledge to be with Joshua and Israel, is also part of a divine war ideology."

God's claim to be with you gives you the umph and power that you will need to do all that He has told you to do. So before you hook up with them, hook up with Him. Joshua, I am accompanying you on this journey. I am running alongside you in this race. I will be among you wherever you go. I will be beside you every step you take. And not only that, I will be upon you. If you want to be successful, make sure God is on your side and God is with you. I understand why Matthew, Mark and Luke tell us that with God all things are possible. Because Romans 8:31 says, *"If God be for us, who can be against us?"*

Dr. D. Featley proclaims that,

"If the Lord thy God Be with Thee; His wisdom is with you to direct you. You have His power to protect you. You have His strength to support you. You have His goodness to maintain you. You have His bounty to reward you. You have His word to encourage you. And if you die under His banner, His angels will show up to carry you into heaven."

The historical record is not just a record of the plan of salvation of God for God's people lead by Joshua. But this record points to the plan of Salvation of God for God's people through Jesus.

Jesus had good success, ask me how he did it. He had concentration: He was focused to do the will of the one that sent Him. He did meditation: He was the Word and the Word was with Him, for He was the lion of the tribe of Judah. Jesus had a roar within Himself. He used observation: He preached to the Word, He lived the Word, He was the Word, and signs and wonders followed His Words. He had the right associations: He said, "I and the father are one, and once you have seen me you have seen the Father."

Jesus had good success. He came not only to seek and save the lost. He came not only to heal the sick and mend the broken hearted. He came not only to heal issues of blood and to bring Lazarus back to life. He came not only to feed thousands with two fish and five loaves. That was a part of His job, but not the reason why He came. So why did He come? He came to be the Lamb that was slain from the foundation of the earth. He came to be despised and rejected, have sorrow and be acquainted with grief. He was oppressed and afflicted, and yet He opened not His mouth. He was taken from prison and from judgment and for His people He was stricken.

Jesus had good success. He successfully took the nails in His hand and His feet. He successfully bore the crown of thorns on His head. He successfully declared it is finished. He successfully snatched the keys of hell, death and the grave. He successfully rose on the third day morning with all power in His hands. He successfully now sits at the right hand of the Father making intercession for you and me. Jesus had good success. He had concentration, He had meditation, He had observation and He had association. And one day He will successfully return and receive us unto Himself. Matthew 25:34 says: *"Then shall the King say unto them on his right hand, Come, ye blessed of my Father, inherit the kingdom prepared for you from the foundation of the world."*

I just want to be successful.

CHAPTER SIX

It's the God in Me

Focal Passage: 1st John 4:1-8 (NIV)

1 John 4 King James Version (KJV)

¹ Beloved, believe not every spirit, but try the spirits whether they are of God: because many false prophets are gone out into the world. ² Hereby know ye the Spirit of God: Every spirit that confesseth that Jesus Christ is come in the flesh is of God: ³ And every spirit that confesseth not that Jesus Christ is come in the flesh is not of God: and this is that spirit of antichrist, whereof ye have heard that it should come; and even now already is it in the world. ⁴ Ye are of God, little children, and have overcome them: because greater is he that is in you, than he that is in the world. ⁵ They are of the world: therefore speak they of the world, and the world heareth them. ⁶ We are of God: he that knoweth God heareth us; he that is not of God heareth not us. Hereby know we the spirit of truth, and the spirit of error. ⁷ Beloved, let us love *one another: for love is of God; and every one that loveth is born of God, and knoweth God. ⁸ He that loveth not knoweth not God; for God is love.*

It would be easy to wake up every morning and do nothing, but you've got to have something on the inside to get up, get dressed and make something of yourself. It would be easy to go to class and never do any work, but you've got to have something on the inside to be the best student you can be. It would be easy to not move on because of fear of the unknown, but you've got to have something on the inside to put fear, insecurity and passivity in its place and go get your life back. It would be easy to blame somebody else for where you are in life, but you've got to have something on the inside to take responsibility for your future and make it happen.

It would be easy to say the dog ate my homework, the car would not start or my wife doesn't cook, but you got to have something on the inside to get your work done, get to work on time and learn how to cook for yourself. It would be easy to get a divorce, look for somebody else, and start dating again, but you've got to have something on the inside to make a non-violent marriage work, get healed from your last relationship and get ready for God to give you what's next.

It would be easy to go to church and think that is enough, but you got to have something on the inside to take what you know about Him and share it with a dying world.

It would be easy to lie down with dogs and get up with fleas, but you got to have something on the inside to say this body is a living sacrifice and when it lies down it is lying down on a honeymoon, and not a one night stand.

It would be easy to walk around clueless about your condition, unconscious about your calamity and checked out of your Christianity, but you've got to have something on the inside to find out and do something about your condition and calamity and to exemplify your Christianity.

You've got to have something on the inside down in you that will show up in the midst of trial and tribulation. Something on the inside that will push you forward when you feel like giving up. Something inside so strong that tells you, you can make it and something better than Nike that will still say, "Just Do It!" Something better than The Secret that will still say, "Just Think It." Something better than Jenny Craig that will still say, "Just Loose It." Something better than Chex Mix that will still say, "Just Try It." Something better than James Brown, that still tells you to "Feel Good." Something better than MC Hammer, which says, "You Can't Touch This." Something better than Stevie Wonder that tells you, "Stay True to Your Heart."

Something better than Lee Harding that will give you, "The Eye of the Tiger." Something better than the Dominoes & Jackie Wilson that will say, "You Can't Keep a Good Man Down." Something better than Whitney Houston that will call Himself, "The Greatest Love of All." Something better than

WILL.I.AM, which will still say, "Yes We Can." Something better than TAG TEAM, that will still say, "Whoomp There it Is."

What is it that some people call inspiration that is the arousal of the mind to special unusual activity or creativity? Some people call it a burst of inner strength that is overcoming a psychological weakness. But I can't call what I feel inspiration or inner strength.

What I feel has to be, for it is light and in it is no darkness. This is faithful and just to forgive me and cleanse me from all of my unrighteousness. This sits and advocates for me. This is the propitiation for my sins and the worlds. It forgives my sins for His name's sake. Its word abides in me. His will abides forever. His anointing teaches me all things.

Something in me I can't explain, but it has not revealed to me what all I shall be, but when it does, I shall be like Him and see Him as He is. It is pure. It was manifested to take away our sins and in Him is no sin. It will not allow me to be deceived. It exposes the works of the devil. It is greater than our heart and knows all things. Something in me I can't explain it, but oh my, it has to be the God in me.

I want to claim John gives three reasons why I know it had to be the God in me. It's the God in me because my response on the other side of belief would have been different.

Verse 1 tells us, *Beloved, believe not every spirit, but try the spirits whether they are of God: because many false prophets are gone out into the world.* I would have followed anybody who told me they knew the way. I would have slept with anybody who told me I was pretty. I would have marched with any group who made me feel special. I would have stayed in every relationship that allowed me to do what I wanted to. I would have watched every reality show that I agreed with. I would have taken every pill they prescribed for my child and me. I would have believed every report about my past. I would have never gone back to college. I would have never looked for a better relationship. It's the God in me, because my response on the other side of belief would have been different.

I would have never cried and thought to myself, my Father has hired servants who eat better than this. I would have never thought to myself, I've got to get away from these pigs. I would have never turned around and went home to my Fathers house. It's the God in me because my response on the other side of Christ would have torn the choir apart, punched out the praise team, chopped up the church meeting and turned over every pew. My response, my actions, my doings and my reactions would have been different on the other side of belief, on the other side of accepting Him as true, genuine and trustworthy. Oh you better be glad you met me on this side because on the other side it would have been different. Thank God now I believe.

It's the God in me because my confession on the other side of Christ would have been crucial.

Verses 2 tells us, *Hereby know ye the Spirit of God: Every spirit that confesseth that Jesus Christ is come in the flesh is of God: 3And every spirit that confesseth not that Jesus Christ is come in the flesh is not of God: and this is that spirit of antichrist, whereof ye have heard that it should come; and even now already is it in the world.*

If not for the God in me, I would have allowed anything to come out of my mouth. I would have cursed out everybody that hurt my feelings. I would have talked back to every person in authority over me. I would have told the state trooper off for pulling me over. I would have let that girl have it in the line at McDonalds. I would have told that teacher off that was calling my child hyperactive. I would have destroyed my mate's confidence, my sister's accomplishments, and my child's inheritance. I would have told the referee off at the last basketball game.

It's the God in me because my confession on the other side of Christ would have been crucial. My tongue was sharp as a knife, fast as an AK-47 and as deadly as a poisonous snake. It's the God in me because my confession, my comments, my disclosures and my declarations on the other side of Christ would have messed you up. But since Christ, my words of choice are silver.

Lastly, God had to be in me not only because my response on the other side of belief would have been different and not only because my confession for Christ would have been crucial. But I know: It's the God in Me because I overcame the opposition of the opponent.

Verse 4 tells us, *Ye are of God, little children, and have overcome them: because greater is he that is in you, than he that is in the world. When the enemies came in and surrounded me, the spirit of the Lord lifted up a standard against. When I had a chance to get revenge on my enemies, I got down on my knees and said, "Father forgive them for they know not what they do." When sickness and disease told me I was one my deathbed, I got a helping hand from the Balm in Gilead.*

When financial burdens emerged around me, I knew that my God would supply all my needs according to His riches in glory. When the job gave me a pink slip, I went out and opened my own business. You are of God's little children, and you have overcome them, and greater is He that is in me than He that is in the world.

I am reminded of David, who in I Samuel 17, went out to fight Goliath. Goliath saw him as a little ruddy boy, in other words, a little child. The Philistines said, "Come to me, and I will give your flesh to the birds of the air and the beasts of the field."

The opponent, Goliath, was big and tall, he was a giant. But David rose up and said, "You come to me with a sword (you have weapons, you come up with my past, you come up with ammunition by attacking my character, you try to convince me that I am not all God called me to be and you try to go off of my last response. You try to bring me out and embarrass me). You come with artillery and a huge army, you come with hostility, you come to start conflict, you come to start a disagreement and you come with great opposition, but I come in the name of the Lord of hosts, the God of the armies of Israel. And this day, the Lord will deliver you into my hands."

And the Bible says that as Goliath ran towards David, David didn't cower, but ran straight towards Goliath and pulled out his sling and one of his five smooth stones. David slung the stone and hit Goliath in the forehead, Goliath fell to the ground and David drew his sword and killed him dead. David, a little boy overcame the opposition of the opponent.

And I want to point out that it was not the smooth stone, it was not the strength of David and it was not his speed as a little boy. But there was something on the inside of David poured on him by Samuel that was ignited by the Holy Ghost, and came out of him on the day he met his opposition. If David could testify today in the sanctuary, he would say, "It's the God in me." Because if God was not in him, his response would have been different.

If God was not in me, my confession would have been crisscrossed and crucial. If God was not in me, I would have been overcome by the opposition of my opponent. I would have allowed what I was facing to trick me out of what I knew about who I am and whose I am. But greater is He that is in me than He that is in the world.

There is something big out there, but there is something bigger in here. There is something trying to get in, but there is something bigger trying to get out. There is a victim out there, but there is a victor in here. Something on the inside, I just can't explain. But I know what's in here is bigger, is greater and is better than what I see out there. Greater is He that is in me than He that is in the world.

CHAPTER SEVEN

Let the Children Testify

Focal Passages: Psalm 8:1-3 & Matthew 21:15-17

Psalm 8 (KJV)

¹ LORD, our Lord, how excellent is thy name in all the earth! who hast set thy glory above the heavens. ² Out of the mouth of babes and sucklings hast thou ordained strength because of thine enemies, that thou mightest still the enemy and the avenger. ³ When I consider thy heavens, the work of thy fingers, the moon and the stars, which thou hast ordained;

Matthew 21:15-17 (KJV)

¹⁵ And when the chief priests and scribes saw the wonderful things that he did, and the children crying in the temple, and saying, Hosanna to the son of David; they were sore displeased, ¹⁶ And said unto him, Hearest thou what these say? And Jesus saith unto them, Yea; have ye never read, Out of the mouth of babes and sucklings thou hast perfected praise? [17] *And he left them, and went out of the city into Bethany; and he lodged there.*

When one testifies, it is an opportunity to make a statement based on personal knowledge or belief. It is an opportunity to give a testimony, a solemn proof of the truth of the matter. In the law, testimony is a form of evidence that is obtained from a witness who makes a solemn statement or declaration of fact. When on the bench of testimony, it is not time to give an opinion based on your perception; it is time to present a fact of what you have seen. It is not the time to state what you think about the matter, it is time to tell the truth.

However in religious experience and expression, the word "testimony" takes on a whole other truth. In religion, *testimony* "involves an inward belief or outward profession of faith or of personal religious experience." Christians use the word "testify" or say "give your testimony" to mean the story of how you became a Christian (or less commonly it may refer to a specific event in a Christian's life in which God has done something deemed particularly worth sharing). In other words, it is your opportunity to tell somebody just how good God has been. And not only that, they testify so that non-believers can hear how God has been at work in the lives of believers.

Oh, you have to be careful when you testify, because testimony does not come from secondhand information, it comes from a witness, somebody that has touched it, seen it, heard it and smelled it firsthand. We need a witness, a bystander, a spectator, a testifier and a watcher. We can't use a denier, a refuter or a complier, we need a witness…can I get a witness?

In the text, we have a witness to the goodness of God. In the text, we have a group of people making a statement about something they have seen for themselves. David is out one clear night while tending sheep in an open field, and begins to declare, what he sees. David testifies, "Oh Lord, our Lord how excellent is thy name in all the earth." He cannot afford to believe secondhand knowledge because telling what somebody else told you might get you in trouble. So he declares, "When I consider thy heavens, the work of thy fingers, the moon and the stars, which thou hast ordained." He has been subpoenaed by the court of praise and questions, "What is man that thou are mindful of him, and the son of man that thou visited him, for thou has made him a little lower than the angels, and crowned him with glory and honor."

Don't get angry at David, he's just testifying to what he sees, what he smells, and of who it is that put him in charge over the works of his hand. But that's not what I want to talk about. There is another group of people testifying, children crying out Hosanna to the Son of David. There is another group who takes the witness stand and bears testimony to what they have seen and heard for themselves. You better be careful of secondhand information, it just might get you in trouble.

This group is testifying, but the problem is they are

children. Now we know that sometimes we don't listen to children. We don't think they know what they are talking about. We think children are supposed to be seen and not heard. We think that they think they know it all. We think that they can't understand us or where we are coming from. We hate it when they do the exact opposite of what we say to them, and then we go back and do the exact opposite of what they say to us. Do you know how many adults are uncomfortable to talk to children?

But this text says they are not just children, but they are suckling babes. They can't even talk at that age, they just scream, and cry and eat, and scream and cry and eat, and say goo-goo, gaga, lady gaga. Mama and Daddy think they just babble and make noise and we think they are just making noise, but they are really having conversations that our ears have not been tuned to understand or interpret.

Medical science shows that babies don't talk until they understand. Babies will babble and make sounds like none other normally until around the sixth month when they begin this process called sound imitation. First, the child repeats the sounds that he makes himself, and then the child repeats what he hears coming from another adult or another child.

That's why we need a witness; we need somebody who will repeat what God has done for them first then what God is doing in someone else. Somebody ought to stand up and testify. Somebody ought to stand up and say something. However the child begins to speak when the child understands.

Here in our text, the children are crying out a prayer, a petition and praise all in one phrase, "Hosanna to the Son of David." They are saying "Oh, save us Son of David and Word of prayer. They are saying Hosanna, in the Greek translated as Yasha na, which in petition means be open wide and free now. They are say Yasha na, which in praise means get the victory now and then.

The children, Matthews calls them, are testifying. They just saw with their own eyes, how Jesus cleaned out the money changers from the temple, and reclaimed the church as the house of prayer for all people. They just saw firsthand how the blind and lame came to him and he healed them of their infirmity. They were eyewitnesses to the facts and gave a testimony. They felt that they ought to say something. Because when God does something for you, the least you can do is tell somebody else what the Lord has done for you.

The song writer said it a little like this, "Said I wasn't going to tell nobody, but I couldn't keep it to myself, I thought about it, prayed about it, had to tell somebody else." Somebody ought to testify.

And in our text the children began to testify. The text tells us what happens when we testify. Not only will people rejoice with you, but the priest may also be displeased with you. The text records that the priests who saw the great things that Jesus had done got angry. Here is the problem, the priests were the authority or rulers of the temple in that time and were responsible for serving as mediator between the people and God. If anybody should have praised, it should have been the priest and the people. Instead, the priest got angry. This helps us understand that just because you've seen it with your own eyes does not mean that you are a witness. The people went to praise and the priests were displeased. The priest also saw it, but had nothing to say about it.

I wonder how many priests we have in the temple, watching the hand of God move that just sit there, not acknowledging God's work, and have the nerve to get angry. They felt something was going wrong. They, if in court, were saying they object to your honor. We speculate that what they are saying is not true. The priests were displeased at the praise of the powerless, but were not displeased when the money changers in the temple were selling lame and blind sacrifices to the worshippers. I ask, are you a priest or a praiser? The people were praising, the children were testifying and the priests who should have lead the praise, were displeased. Let the children testify. Let them say something!

Note on children: Medical science also shows that if a child does not speak after a certain time, the first thing you should check is their hearing. Hearing is very specific.

The priests in the text are angry and raise a question to Jesus, the Messiah and great teacher. Don't you hear what they are saying? They wanted to know if Jesus had turned a deaf ear to the testimony of His people. But they must have forgotten that

Jesus supplied the Blood of the Lamb and was the testimony they spoke of. They forgot that the testimony of Jesus is the spirit of prophecy. They forgot that he that believeth on the Son of God hath the witness in himself.

The priests wanted to check the hearing of Jesus, but Jesus checked their reading. He says to them, *"Have you not read, Mr. Teacher, that out of the mouths of babes and suckling thou hast perfected praise?"* Jesus is saying here, I know you have read all the scripture. I know you are in the place of power, I know that you have always lived right and never made a mistake. I know you have power and status. I know you have a priestly garment and a prophetic utterance, but the problem is your power has blocked you from having a place for praise.

Have you not read out of the mouths of babes and sucklings, those who can barely walk, and those who can barely talk? Out of the mouths of babes, those who are powerless and in need of a mother's milk each day? Out of the mouths of babes, those who keep trying to get up and stumble back down to the ground? Out of the mouths of babes, those who have to crawl sometimes run into a road block? Out of the mouths of babes, those who have to depend on me every step of the way? They may not have power, but they have one thing, they have a place for my praise to be perfected in them.

The Greek word for *perfected* is "katartizo," which means to "complete thoroughly, i.e. repair, or adjust, fit, frame, mend, make perfect." They have a place for my praise to make them perfect. My praise fits them. My praise repairs them. My praise mends them. Let the children testify. Somebody ought to say something. Are their any babies in the house? Not just those young in age, but those who recognize they still have a lot of growing up to do. Somebody ought to say something.

Remember the science, if the child is not speaking, the first thing you should check is their hearing? Now I understand why the Bible says that faith comes by hearing and hearing by the Word of God. How shall they hear without a preacher, and how can he preach unless he is sent? Do you not know? Have you not heard? Has it not been told to you from the beginning? Have you not understood since the earth was founded? The Lord is the everlasting God, the Creator of the ends of the earth. He will not grow tired or weary, and His understanding no one can fathom. Check your hearing; somebody's crying out He's great and greatly to be praised. You can't afford to be quiet, testify. Tell somebody.

Luke puts a spin on this same story as Jesus was coming down to the place called the Mount of Olives on the way to Jerusalem, the people who had witnessed the great things He had done were crying out in testimony, Blessed is He who comes in the name of the Lord. The Pharisees right there asked Jesus to tell His disciples to be quiet, and Jesus said, *"If these be quiet, the very rocks will begin to cry out."* (Luke 19:28-44)

And if the songwriter were here, they would say I don't want any rocks crying out for me.

But there was a day when the rocks began to cry out. The Bible says it was at the moment when Jesus said, *"Father, into thy hand I commend my spirit,"* and he gave up the ghost and died. And in Matthew 27:51-53, at the moment Jesus dies, a massive earthquake strikes and opens tombs where dead people rise again. The earth began to testify so much that the dead got up out of their graves. I call it the place of perfected praise. It was a praise that brought lives back together again. It was a praise that mended spirit and flesh. It was a testimony that caused that which was dead and over to live and start anew. Somebody ought to say something. But one day soon and very soon, the dead in Christ shall rise and those of us that remain and are caught up to meet Him in the air will testify to His greatness. Witness. Testify. Let the children testify.

CHAPTER EIGHT

Speak Up for Your Sons

Focal Passage: Matthew 3:16-17; Mark 1:9-11;
Luke 3:21-22

Matthew 3:16-17 New King James Version (NKJV)

16 When He had been baptized, Jesus came up immediately from the water; and behold, the heavens were opened to Him, and He[a] saw the Spirit of God descending like a dove and alighting upon Him. 17 And suddenly a voice came from heaven, saying, "This is My beloved Son, in whom I am well pleased."

Mark 1:9-11 New King James Version (NKJV)

9 It came to pass in those days that Jesus came from Nazareth of Galilee, and was baptized by John in the Jordan. 10 And immediately, coming up from[a] the water, He saw the heavens parting and the Spirit descending upon Him like a dove.

[11]{.superscript} Then a voice came from heaven, "You are My beloved Son, in whom I am well pleased."

Luke 3:21-22 New King James Version (NKJV)

[21] When all the people were baptized, it came to pass that Jesus also was baptized; and while He prayed, the heaven was opened. [22] And the Holy Spirit descended in bodily form like a dove upon Him, and a voice came from heaven which said, "You are My beloved Son; in You I am well pleased."

At the end of 2011, Verizon Wireless was noted as the largest wireless communications services provider in the United States having over 108.7 million subscribers. They offer wireless voice, messaging and data products and services to customers in the United States. In 2002, Verizon Wireless adopted the slogan, "We Never Stop Working for You," with commercials depicting a Verizon employee roaming about in strange places continuously asking, "Can you hear me now? Good."

The "employee" is played by stage actor, Paul Marcarelli, and as the "test man," he represents Verizon technicians. When the commercials would come on, you saw the "test man" caught in the strangest of places and asking the question to the person on the cellular device, "Can you hear me now? Good." He was seen in the desert, "Can you hear me now? Good." He was seen in the busy city streets of large cities, "Can you hear me now? Good." The test man was seen riding on a bus with sleeping man snoring on his shoulder, "Can you hear me now? Good."

Theses commercials were designed to prove that no matter where you were, the service that Verizon provided allowed you to make a call, receive a call, hear a call and stay connected. "Can you hear me now? Good." For the customer, it is extremely important to invest in a service that allows you, no matter where you are, to be able to make and receive a call, but more importantly, to hear the call clearly.

People hate it, when a call is dropped. But it's worse, when the reception is so poor that you can't hear what the other person is saying. They adjust the volume but still can't hear, sometimes it's too loud and they can't hear. Then they move themselves to another place, where they can finally hear and then the call drops or they loose the signal. The network promises to allow you to make a call from wherever you are. When the network or it's device does not provide what they promise, you best believe that as soon as that person gets a signal, or under the guise of coverage the network supposedly provides, they will be on the customer service provider's line, raising cane in complaint because they are paying for something they can't use, is inoperative or because they simply can't hear.

People need to hear. When you need directions and are trying to get them from someone over your phone, but bad reception doesn't allow you to hear, you get lost. When you get lost, you get frustrated. When you get frustrated, you forget that you are a member of God's church and say the wrong thing.

People get mad when they can't hear.

When you can't hear, you start to guess what was said and end up all messed up. People get mad when they can't hear. It's not that the other person is not saying anything; it may be just the fact that you are using a device, a mechanism or system that is not allowing you to hear what is being said. And when you can't hear you yell out, "speak louder" or "I can't hear you."

We find ourselves in a particular place in the sacred text where there is a 400 year span of time between Malachi 4:6 and Matthew 1:1, where no Prophetic voice has been heard and there was no record of anyone calling up the service provider with a complaint.

What happens when God ceases to speak and nobody complains? What happens when Word no longer flows from the fountain and nobody seems to notice? 400 years is a long time not to hear from heaven, and no one seems to care. 400 years is a long time to be caught in a waiting pattern, looking for permission to go ahead and there is nothing. 400 years is a long time to not have any words from a higher place, with a preview on your life that is not expressed because of where you are. 400 years is a long time to chew on what was said in the past with nothing to push you and propel you to your future.

How do you live with everybody around you saying where you have been but have no idea of where you are going? What happens when there is no Word from the Lord? The temple is there, but God is not. The prophets are there, but God is not. The

King is there, but God is not. The Levites are there, but God is not. We open the text to 400 years of silence.

Silence: no sound, no communication. When things are silent, you are left up to your own devices. Silence can be interpreted as positive or negative. Silence can mean everything and nothing all at the same time. Silence can mean "I trust you," or "you heard what I said," or even "don't move." Silence can mean "no," and silence can mean "make up your own mind." Silence can mean, I'm listening to you," or like the old folk would say, "If you can't say anything nice, don't say anything at all."

The people are in a place where the abode of God, known as heaven is shut up and no heavenly voice can be heard. They can't find anybody with a testimony to share.

Matthew opens the text with the people waiting on a King to establish a kingdom. They are looking for a Messiah to deliver them from a Roman oppressor. They are looking for something to lean on and believe in. But they don't know if they have what they need, because God is silent.

In the first 17 verses, we meet 46 people whose lifetime spans 2,000 years, all ancestors of Jesus. But they don't know if they have what they need, because God is silent. Matthew tells them an angel appears to his earthly father encouraging him to marry the Virgin Mary. For what is coming is of the Holy Ghost, and they are still waiting. But they don't know if they have what they need, because God is silent.

Born in the town of Bethlehem and called the King of the Jews while the King Herod is still reigning, He was visited by wise men who saw a message in the stars and came to worship, and they were still waiting. But they don't know if they have what they need, because God is silent.

Matthew told them He had an all-points-bulletin, APB out on His life, carried to Egypt by His father and mother, taken back to the land of Israel after His pursuers were dead and lived in a town called Nazareth. Making it known that He was the fulfillment of the prophecies of old. And the people were still waiting. But they don't know if they have what they need, because God is silent.

Matthew records how His cousin showed up with a message from heaven, shouting in the wilderness, that the Lord is on His way. And the people were making up their own minds and getting baptized. Even the snakes were getting baptized. But yet they were still waiting. But they don't know if they have what they need, because God is silent.

Matthew records how Jesus, Himself, went from the town of Galilee, without a word from the Lord, showed up at the Jordan, turned away from the baptismal waters by a Baptist Pastor named John. Then Jesus demanded to be baptized, without a word from the Lord and He went down in the water. And still no word from the Lord. Came up out of the waters and right there the windows of heaven opened up and he saw the spirit of God descend like a dove and settling on him. And right then, God breaks the silence and the Bible records, *"And a voice from heaven said 'This is My Beloved Son, in whom I am well pleased.'"* And it was said right in front of everyone so that all could know and see that God was still in the speaking business. But what God says I find of particular importance on this wonderful day and occasion. God Himself decides to speak up for His Son. It teaches us three things for the relevance of our contemporary lives: When you speak up for your sons, you decrease public speculation and you increase personal association.

Matthew's text records in verse 17, *"And a voice from Heaven said, 'This is my beloved Son, in whom I am well pleased.'"* In Matthew's text, the concern was for the growing church, where Jesus had come from, so Matthew spends time from Chapter one all the way to Chapter 3 trying to help us to understand who Jesus was and where He came from, and to whom He belonged.

Everybody in town had ideas about where He came from and to whom He belonged. Some asked how a virgin could have a baby; others said they had the baby in the back of the Holiday Inn. And that He was the son of a no backbone father. But that was all speculation. And speculation is a message expressing an opinion based on incomplete evidence.

Speculation is guesswork, a notion or an assumption. Speculation is a shot in the dark. It's close, but it's not the truth. So God decides to do away with all of the guesswork and declare, "This is my Son." God understood that if you let the crowd talk too much for too long, you might begin to believe what they say about your Son.

Might this be a message to us to not allow our sons to go too long with incomplete evidence of the crowd and stand up and say you may have the facts but you don't know the truth? And the truth is that He is not out there all by Himself, this is my Son. He may be struggling right now, but this is my Son. He may be in trouble right now, but this is my Son. He may be a little rough around the edges, but this is my Son. And when you decrease public speculation you increase personal association.

God is not only calling Jesus His Son, but here He is publicly stating that, "we are connected together." We are in partnership, and have a common purpose and interest. We are linked together. God the Father is not only declaring Jesus as Son, He is saying, "And what ever he does, it is a reflection of who He is connected to." Now I can understand why Jesus says throughout the Gospel once you have seen Me, you have seen the Father. Because when you speak up for your sons, you decrease public speculation and you increase personal association.

Maybe we should publicly tell the crowd that our Sons are publicly reinforced by our connection to them and say out loud that what you do is a reflection of who I am. People ought to be able to look at you and say you look just like your daddy!

Not only does speaking up for your sons decrease public speculation and increase personal association but, when you speak up for your sons, you magnify identification over realization.

Mark's text records in verse 11, *"And a voice came from heaven, You are my Son, the beloved, with you I am well pleased."* The voice declares that you are mine and I am pleased with you. It brings me to some questions, because Jesus has not done anything yet, but God is pleased. I know that baptism is significant, however there is no record that Jesus has done anything substantial as recorded in any of the Gospel, but be born and carried on a conversation with the religious leaders in the temple, which got him in trouble and the Bible says that God says I am pleased with you!

Maybe God is trying to help us understand that we can't wait until they accomplish something that is pleasing to everyone else, that we decide to take ownership of them and celebrate them. Maybe God is teaching us to see them as He sees them, before they manifest anything pleasing to us. Jesus is at the beginning of His ministry and has not preached one sermon, healed one person, cast out one demon or forgiven one iniquity, yet God starts off the celebration with a commendation.

God gives the first endorsement and God gives the first approval rating. However God identifies Him from a place not of momentary celebration. God says you are mine, and the emphasis here is in the Greek word "mine" a prolongation of the word "my," meaning the "act of continuing an activity without interruption." God is pleased not because of any accomplishment that Jesus will do in the future, but He is pleased because Jesus is His, regardless of what He does and that will be the case without interruption.

Could God be teaching us to take care of them, speak up for them and be responsible for them regardless of what they do or don't do? God celebrates the identification over the realization. God celebrates Jesus regardless of the ups and downs He will face. God celebrates Jesus just because He belongs to Him. What will happen in your life when you understand that God holds you in the palm of His hand uninterrupted? That God is going to keep on making a way for you regardless? That God will uphold you and not let you fall? Would you come out of sin, if you really got it that the Great I am is happy to help you through? Would you stop turning your back on God, if you really knew that He would be there when your world is on fire? That He will lead you to a safe place, even if you loose the game? What will happen with our sons, if they knew that win or loose, they still had a home to go to? What would happen with our sons if they knew that there is a place for them if they just would come back home?

God says, "This is my beloved Son in whom I am well pleased." When you speak up for your sons, you magnify identification over realization. They don't have to be finished yet, they still belong to me. Why? Because, He that hath begun a good work in us shall surely perform it until the day of Jesus Christ. (Phillipians1:6) And God has already said well done because He knows the end and the beginning.

When you speak up for your sons, not only will you decrease public speculation and increase personal association, not only will it magnify identification over realization, but lastly, when you speak up for your sons, it gives them parental affirmations that will sustain them through Satan's temptations.

Luke's text records a voice that came from heaven and said, *"You are my beloved Son, in whom I am well pleased."* Verse 23 says that Jesus was about 30-years-old when He began his work. And Luke 1: 4 tells us that Jesus, full of the Holy Ghost, returned from the Jordan and was led by the spirit into the wilderness where He would be tempted by the devil.

When Jesus has to go up against His first big trial, He does not go alone; for He goes with the affirmation of His Father.

Remez Sasson:

"Affirmations are positive statements that describe a desired situation, and which are repeated many times, in order to impress the subconscious mind and trigger it into positive action. In order to ensure the effectiveness of the affirmations, they have to be repeated with attention, conviction, interest and desire."

It was something said to Him by a parent that sustains Him as He goes to face His giant. However, the words here are not the words of His mother, for in Hebrew culture, the words of a mother to a son were just echoed words that came from the father. In Hebrew culture, it was the father's responsibility to provide guidance, sustenance, protection and direction for the family. The father had the right to arrange and cancel the plans of his children. He could set them up for a life of success, or sell them into a system of servitude. The father had to speak over the son before the son was released into society and ultimately here into battle. The father is the source that sustains, protects, nourishes and provides identity for that which he produces. So whatever the father teaches the mother echoes.

However in our current day, we have sons who are so mixed up because they are receiving two different messages, possibly because some earthly fathers are out of place and off course. If the son is going to be successful in the battle to come, there must be in his life the voice of the Father and the echo of the mother. Momma can't start it; she has got to echo it. Here Jesus is at the inauguration of His public ministry and His first stop is the wilderness to be tempted by the devil. But it was the Words of His Father that sustained Him and gave Him the victory over the devil. So much so that Satan had to go away and strategize how he would try to catch Jesus off guard.

Ramez Sasson:

"Words and statements work at both ways, to build or destroy. It is the way we use them that determines whether they are going to bring good or harmful results."

Could God be sharing that secret with us? That what we put in our sons ought to be able to help them fight off the devil when they are out there in this world all by themselves? When we speak up for our sons, it gives them parental affirmations that will sustain them through Satan's temptations.

Tell our sons who they are so that when they are not in our presence they will reflect who we are to the world. Don't tell them statistics, but the truth about their inheritance. Don't let the public speculate over them. Stand and declare that this is my beloved son, in whom I am well pleased. They are connected. They are the trees of righteousness. They are blessed and highly favored.

They are what God says they are. Tell them, that you think well of them. Don't let society define your child as a thug, you clarify, and say that's my son. Don't let your girlfriends define your husband, you clarify, and say that's my man of God. Don't let the streets and gangs have your children, you clarify, and say those are my children. Don't let the enemy snatch your children away from you, you clarify, and say they are mine. They might not be much to you, but they belong to me. Don't let the television raise your children, you clarify, and say that's my child. This is my beloved son, in whom I am well pleased.

In our text, He is not just the Son of righteousness with healing in His wings. And this is not just the moment of His inauguration as He goes forth into His public ministry.

But Matthew, Mark and Luke agree that the language used here is not just the Endorsement of a Father over an obedient Son, but also the allusion leading to the surrender of a suffering servant. They all agree that in the Old Testament there are two records where God said, "In you I am well pleased."

Psalm 2:6 talks about the coming King and Isaiah 42:1 says the pleasure of God is a subjugated servant. It's a Son that has to go into the wilderness and gain victory over Satan. But it is a servant that has to go to the cross of Calvary.

It is a Son that has to remember the teachings of His Father. But it is a servant that has to say, "Not my will, but thy will be done."

It is a Son that has to declare, "Man does not live by bread alone, but by every word that proceeds out of the mouth." But a servant has to declare, "Father forgive them for they know not what they do." It is a Son that says, "And He will give his angels charge over you, and they will bear you up, that your foot will not dash the stone." But it is a suffering servant that says, "Father, why has thou forsaken me?"

It is a celebrated Son that says, "Do not put the Lord your God to the test." But it is a suffering servant that says, "Woman behold your Son and Son Behold your mother, It is a celebrated Son that says, "Man shall not live by bread alone but by every word that proceeds out of the mouth of God," but it is a suffering servant that says "I assure you today you will be with me in paradise."

It is a celebrated son that says, "Away with you Satan, for it is written, worship the Lord your God and serve him only." But it is a suffering servant that says, "It is finished."

And He died. He died until the world was notified, sinners

got justified, hearts got purified, hell was horrified and heaven was glorified. He died. I said, "He died."

But early Sunday morning, He got up with all power in His Hand. It was a Son that got the victory over the devil in the wilderness, but it was the servant that got the victory over hell, death and the grave. And they both hear the same words, *"This is my Beloved Son in whom I am well pleased!"* Whether you are the celebrated son or the suffering servant, God says He is well pleased.

Let me tell you how important a father's words are. As I was jogging one morning, I saw something strange to me. It was a man with a stroller pushing a child down the street and he was looking down into the stroller as he pushed forward. And as I got closer, I could hear him talking and the closer I got, the more I could hear what he was saying. I slowed up and saw that he was talking to his daughter, she was just an infant and she was laid back with the canopy pulled over to block the morning sunlight.

And the father was telling the little girl, "Look baby, that's Howard, you know Daddy went to Howard, and you are going to go to Howard too, that's right, Howard." And I told him, "That's right Dad, tell her." And he smiled and kept on going.

I was so excited to see a father pushing his baby down the street and telling her where she was going in her future. But as I kept on jogging, I reflected and I noticed that the baby was listening and just riding along. Laid back and just riding. Although the canopy was covering her view of her father, it didn't seem to affect her. And the Holy Ghost said she was able to keep riding in comfort, because she was so near to the father's voice. And sometimes when you can't see Him, you've got to stay close enough to hear His voice and keep on riding.

CHAPTER NINE

Wake Up Little Girl!

Focal Passage: Mark 5:35-43 (KJV)

35 While he yet spake, there came from the ruler of the synagogue's house certain which said, Thy daughter is dead: why troublest thou the Master any further? 36 As soon as Jesus heard the word that was spoken, he saith unto the ruler of the synagogue, Be not afraid, only believe. 37 And he suffered no man to follow him, save Peter, and James, and John the brother of James. 38 And he cometh to the house of the ruler of the synagogue, and seeth the tumult, and them that wept and wailed greatly. 39 And when he was come in, he saith unto them, Why make ye this ado, and weep? the damsel is not dead, but sleepeth. 40 And they laughed him to scorn. But when he had put them all out, he taketh the father and the mother of the damsel, and them that were with him, and entereth in where the damsel was lying. 41 And he took the damsel by the hand, and said unto *her, Talitha cumi; which is, being interpreted, Damsel, I say unto thee, arise. ⁴² And straightway the damsel arose, and walked; for she was of the age of twelve years. And they were astonished with a great astonishment. ⁴³ And he charged them straitly that no man should know it; and commanded that something should be given her to eat.*

(NLT) ⁴¹ Holding her hand, he said to her, "Talitha koum," which means "Little girl, get up!"

The Gospel according to Mark tells the good news about Jesus. For Mark, Jesus is a man of action and authority. Jesus is the Son of Man, who came to give His life to set people free from sin. Mark focuses on what Jesus does: Jesus heals, Jesus teaches and Jesus is a doer, not just a talker. Mark lets people know that Jesus will do something about your problem. He will speak, but that is not all, unlike many others who have something to say about what you are going through, Jesus comes to say and do something about it.

In the focal text, we find Jesus doing something. What He does is of focus because the good news is that when Jesus shows up He acts with authority and power. Jesus is found in the text, casting legions of demons out of a man whose possessors caused a herd of pigs to jump over the cliff and drown themselves in a lake. Jesus is asked to leave the area for causing a major decrease in sales and revenue which changed the economic status of pig herders who are more concerned about their own economic stability than the deliverance of a demon possessed brother bound for better days.

As Jesus leaves and moves into another area, an official of the local synagogue arrives and begs Jesus to come see his little girl who at this point is sick. He begs Jesus to do something. He says, "Come and place Your hands on her, so that she will get well and live." Whatever the little girl is facing, the father is convinced that Jesus can do something about it. And consistent with the Markan theme, Jesus moves in the direction of the ruler Jarius' house. While on the way, the crowd grows and someone from within the crowd reaches out and pulls power and virtue out of Jesus. And Jesus is not the only one doing something, a woman with an issue of blood also does something that changes her life and grabs the attention of the Master Teacher Himself. (Maybe, instead of us waiting for God to do everything for us, we may need to stand up with His guidance and power and do something for ourselves.)

While confirming the healing of the woman who was made whole, the brother with the sick daughter gets a message from home that the daughter is now dead. Jesus acts real cool and tells the brother who did something about his daughter's problem to not be afraid, but only believe. So Jesus resumes the trip.

Isn't it amazing how Jesus can hear the facts about your situation and still walk towards you with the truth? They said she was dead and there was no need for Jesus to come any further. But when Jesus has something to do in your life, even what "they said," will not stop him. He kept on going. When they arrived at the home, the mourners were already at her bedside. Jesus said, "Why are you crying? The child is not dead, she is only sleeping." The people started making fun of Him so Jesus decided to send them all outside and called for the father, mother and his three disciples to stay in the room where the girl was lying. Mark 5: 41 tells us He took her by the hand and said to her, *"Talitha Cumi,"* which means, "wake up, little girl."

There are a few things I would like to investigate in the text. I would like to ask, what was it that put her to sleep? Now the people who got there before Jesus knew she was dead. But when Jesus arrived, He says she is only asleep. Everybody's tears express that this is a time of mourning and grief, but another man, one man by Himself, says this is a time of rest and revitalization. The people from the crowd say that this girl is finished, dead. And the prophet who was just put out of another town for doing miracles says this is just a pause in the promise.

Now I am not the smartest man, but I know there is a difference between someone being dead and someone being asleep. When someone is dead they have expired, checked out, pushed up the daises, are resting in peace, have gone to meet their maker and are no more. When someone is dead they are no longer living; bereft of sensation, lacking sensitivity, incapable of being emotionally moved, no longer functioning, they can't feel, they can't move, they don't speak, are not fruitful and have no bounce or resilience; they are tasteless and dead as a flat

Pepsi Cola. But when someone is asleep they are in a period of dormancy and inactivity. To be asleep is to be careless and unalert. To be asleep is to suspend consciousness. To be asleep is to be at times lethargic, disinterested, idle, inactive, slothful, unconcerned and unmindful. Let's say that again: to sleep is to suspend consciousness.

Now there is a difference between someone being asleep and being dead. But since I'm a Christian preacher, I'm going to go with Jesus and say she was asleep. And Jesus walked into the room, took the little girl's hand and said, but wait, Jesus, wait. I have a question before we complete this verse. What made the little girl go to sleep?

What made this little girl who was at one time awake, alert, responsive, and sensible, become inattentive, indifferent, impassive and unintentional. Jesus I really want to ask you this question; what caused her to suspend consciousness? What caused her to hang up on life, lay aside her own convictions, put an end to her own point of view, boycott her own suspicions and abandon her own vision? Jesus I need some help to understand why this little girl suspended consciousness. Can you tell me what put her to sleep?

And for us Jesus, "What is putting our girls to sleep?" Maybe she was listening to Rihanna and asked for a Rude Boi, who can take it and love her. Rihanna wants somebody to be the captain instead of holding on to her convictions of what a real relationship is all about. Can you tell me what put this little girl to sleep? Maybe it was the constant bass heard coming from a low-rider that came with the understanding that if you're going to be my girl, you got to do what I say and give it up when I want it. Maybe she put aside her own point of view just to ride in a car with rims and be seen by her friends. Can you please tell me what put her to sleep?

Maybe it was the voice of a little brother who spent more time with her than her own father, and now he has convinced her to quit college and work to support a habit on inner city corners, neglecting the voice of a caring mother who gave all she had to send her to school. Can you tell me what is putting our girls to sleep? Maybe it was communication given to her about her body that made her feel better about herself because no one ever talked to her about personal growth and development. When this inappropriate orientation comes to her she suspends the possibility of purity until marriage and becomes a misfit on Myspace, a talk around town through texting, a fresh catch on Facebook. She becomes indifferent and inattentive to her own well being and strong family and church values. Can you tell me what is putting our girls to sleep?

Our girls, why do they feel like they must expose all to possess all? Why do they feel like they've got to do what they've got to do, why do they feel all alone and want to be strong? Who put this little girl to sleep? But Jesus comes not to answer questions today, He is the answer. Jesus comes to take this little girl by the hand and says, *"Talitha Cumi."* which means, "wake up, little girl." Wake Up. I know you dropped-off but wake up. I know you fell asleep but wake up. I know you slumbered, but wake up, I know you hit the snooze button, but wake up. I know you fell into a trance, but wake up.

The Bible says Jesus grabs her hand and says, "Wake up little girl."

But one more question, Jesus, why was it necessary for this little girl to wake up? The Bible, in verses 22-23, says her father Jarius came to Jesus. He understood that if his daughter was going to get some help, he as a parent had to get to Jesus. She had parents who loved her. Jarius was a ruler of the synagogue who should have had no dealing with Jesus. But he loved his daughter more than his job. He loved his daughter more than his title. And is there a greater way a man can express his love for his family than by putting his needs above his interests? He loved his daughter. That's why she had to get up. She had somebody that was responsible for her to get her circumstance to Jehovah Rapha.

Now I heard of mommas crying over their children, but when you get a father that will get up in the middle of the night, when you have a father that will get off his job and put aside his agenda to see about his child, you, like Jarius, can get God's attention. One man in the Bible said, "Lord, if You just speak a word, my servant will be made whole." But Jarius said Lord if You just come by my house and lay Your hands on my child, I know she will get well and live. He was saying I know she will wake up.

And some parent in here today has been trying to do it on their own, but you ought to get to a place where you say, Lord stop by and lay your hands on my child. I know they will get well and live. And He will stop by and say wake up little girl, wake up little boy. She had to wake up. She had to get up. She had some parents who loved her.

Secondly, I would like to extract a reason in the fact that she had people who pronounced death over her. In verse 35, the people from the house sent the message that the little girl was dead. And if you are not careful you will let people talk you out of your own life. The people will say you will never get better. The people said you were checked out, expired and no more. But you have to be careful because people will call dead what God calls alive. The people will say it looks lifeless, that it has no blood in it and it has gone stiff and ceased to live. She had to wake up because people cannot have the final say over your life. Stop living by what people say and start living by what God says about you. People will praise you today and stab you in the back tomorrow.

Be like Paul and ask the Lord to deliver you from people. Here in this text, Mark lets us know that people cannot pronounce death on you when the Messiah is with you. She had to wake up, because to people she looked dead. Because to people she acted dead. Because to people she seemed dead. Because to people she lay dead. Because to people she was dead. But Mark tells us that the Son of Man, who came to die to set us free, also has the power and the authority to make people be a lie and the power of God to be the truth. She had to wake up because the people pronounced death over her. And God had to prove them wrong. She had to wake up.

May I also suggest that she had a Jesus encounter? Verse 41 says when Jesus went in the room; He took her by the hand and said to her, *"Talitha Cumi,"* which means, "wake up, little girl." The little girl had to meet Jesus for herself. So many times we think that the prayers and works of our parents alone will get us into a relationship with Jesus. But let me serve notice, today, you've got to meet him for yourself. In this text, the mourner's tears did not wake her up. In this text, the wailer's wails did not wake her up. In this text, the scorners of Jesus did not wake her up. They put everybody out, but she did not wake up. They walked in the room together, but the little girl did not wake up. They gathered around her death bed, but the little girl did not wake up. The parents finally got Jesus in the room, but the little girl did not wake up. The parents finally got some disciples of Jesus in the room and she did not get up. Jesus reached up and grabbed her hand but she did not wake up.

And some of us come to church and still sleep. Some of us sing in the choir and are still asleep. Some of us teach Sunday school and still sleep. Some of us preach, pray and cry and still sleep. Jesus is in the room and you still sleep. Jesus grabs your hand and you still sleep. But this little girl, when she hears the voice of the Savior for herself saying wake up little girl, the Bible says she got up at once and walked around.

And if you are reading this today, the Lord is calling to you. Wake up, little girl, wake up, little boy, wake up. If you can hear His voice, you better get up, and the Bible says she walked around. Now I understand why the old sanctified church mothers and fathers, used to get out of their seats and walk around, and run around the sanctuary. Because when you hear the voice of Jesus, you can't just sit there like He's not talking to you. When you hear the Holy Ghost of God, you can't just sit there and ignore Him. You have to get up and walk around. Not to please people, not to be seen by men, but because you heard something from the Son of Man. Hallelujah.

She had to wake up, because she had a Jesus to encounter. She had to know Him for herself. And now she can sing, "This joy that I have, the world did not give it to me, and the world can't take it away." She had to know Him for herself. And now she can say in the words of Billie Holiday, "Momma may have, and poppa may have, but God blesses the child that got own her own." She had to know Him for herself. And now she can sing from the hymn, "I was sinking deep in sin, far from the peaceful shore, very deeply stained within, sinking to rise no more, but the master of the seas heard my despairing cry and from the waters He lifted me. Now safe am I." (Love Lifted Me).

She had to wake up, not only because her parents loved her, not only because she had people pronounce death over her and not only because she had a Jesus to encounter. But lastly she had to wake up because: she had another meal coming to her.

In verse 43, Jesus gives her parents strict orders to give her something to eat. Jesus knew she had to go back out there with all the people that said she was dead. Jesus knew that she had to walk among those who thought it was over for her. Jesus knew she had to walk among the enemies of her destiny. So He withdrew from the Hebrew Scriptures that said, *"Thou hast prepared a table before me in the presence of my enemies,"* (Psalm 23) She had to wake up because she had another meal coming to her. And whenever you take in a meal, it is designed to restore that which has been lost and to prepare you for that which is to come. I want to strongly suggest that she had to get up, not only to recover from what she lost, but also to get her ready for what was to come. She had to wake up because she had a future before her.

So I encourage all of my little sisters and brothers, hear the voice of the Lord today and wake up. God has something more for you to do. God has another assignment for your life. They said you were dead, they said it was not hope for you. They said you were as hopeless as a penny with a hole in it, but the Son of Man has stopped by today to wake you up, I have a future for you. *"Eyes have not seen, ears have not heard. No mind has ever imagined what God has prepared for those who love Him,"* (1st Corinthians 2:9 KJ21) *"'For I know the plans I have for you,' declares the Lord, 'plans to prosper you and not to harm you,*

plans to give you hope and a future,'" (Jeremiah 29:11 KJV)
Wake up little girl. Now give her something to eat!

CHAPTER TEN

Who's Child is This?

Focal Passage: Luke 7:31-35 (AMP)

31 So to what shall I compare the men of this generation? And what are they like? 32 They are like little children sitting in the marketplace, calling to one another and saying, We piped to you [playing wedding], and you did not dance; we sang dirges and wailed [playing funeral], and you did not weep. 33 For John the Baptist has come neither eating bread nor drinking wine, and you say, He has a demon. 34 The Son of Man has come eating and drinking, and you say, Behold, a Man Who is a glutton and a wine drinker, a friend of tax collectors and notorious sinners. 35 Yet wisdom is vindicated (shown to be true and divine) by all her children [Lby their life, character, and deeds].

Most of the time you can look at a child and outwardly determine who the parents are. Some children have the same facial features as their parents' eyes, nose, forehead, cheekbones and even mouth structure. But there are others times when you visit the maternity ward at the hospital and all those who have gathered to view the newborn have to point out someone's child to you. They say, "There he is," And you, because you know what the parents allegedly look like start pointing at all the wrong babies on the row. Only the baby they are pointing out does not look like the parents that celebrate its arrival.

As a child grows, most of the time you can watch some of their mannerisms and determine who their parents are. Sometimes it is the way they hold their hands or rub their ears. The food they eat and the food they push away may be indicators of parental charge. You can even watch some of the habits these toddlers have to identify their parents. My nephew wants to do everything himself. Please do not help him with anything. He can do it. Don't even touch it! Or he will give off this noise in another language that is interpreted as, "I can do it myself." Now this action is familiar, because his father wants to do everything by himself. Make it by himself. Discover it by himself. Handle it by himself. Spend it by himself, but only with your money. And if you help him, he gives off this little grunt just like his son, until it is something, he cannot do by himself.

Not only can you identify children by their habits and familiar characteristics or traits that they have inherited from their parents, but you can also determine who people are by their features and the habits they have picked up from their parents and those who have made substantial deposits of time into their development.

Luke, the beloved physician, records the beginning stages and occurrences in the ministry of Jesus. Luke shows us that Jesus is not only a babe born through supernatural causes, but also a bar breaker for people who have been wounded by this matrix called life. Luke proves to us that Jesus is not only a man-child, but also a mighty man of valor who takes time to deal with the disenfranchised and the ostracized and the downtrodden.

Luke paints this picture of a Jesus who is not only a Savior, but a sensor of human emotion betrayed by the lack of sensitivity in human society. Luke records the life of not only a man, but a minister, who came not to be served, but to serve this present age and demonstrate His calling to fulfill.

Luke writes for our viewing and put on display Jesus, not only as a teacher in the temple, but also as a man tender to the touch of plain people. Luke's Jesus is the Christ, but is also compassionate. Luke's Jesus is connected to the Father but is also a friend to fugitives, a playmate to the dropped, a schoolmate to the displaced and a bedfellow to the leper. Luke's Jesus is a roommate to the reprobate, a soul mate to the tramp, a sidekick to the vagabond and a well-wisher to the wretch.

This attitude towards people would possibly help us to identify people who have been called to ministry. Does your preacher hang out with outcasts? Does your leader spend time with people who don't meet your criteria? Do you deal with those who don't believe what you believe?

Jesus proves to us that association does not bring on assimilation as long as you know who you are and whose you are and somebody has spent a substantial amount of time with you who is putting the things of God in you and speaking the Word over you. You can go anywhere, hang with anybody and befriend anyone. The only thing that is at stake is your reputation. Your reputation is what people think about you and your character is what God knows about you. And we must ask the question, whose child is this?

Luke seeks to prove to us that Jesus is connected to the Father by what He does and not necessary what He looks like, the length of His hair, the color of His skin, the wideness of His nose, and the size of His ministry. This identification is not based on what Jesus has but Jesus is identifiable to Luke by what He does.

However, in this particular text Luke records Jesus' ability to identify and discern the mentality and the vitality, and the child-like behavior patterns of the men of this generation compared to the witness of those who dine daily at the breast of wisdom.

In our text, Jesus is confronted by a few of John's disciples. For they have had an opportunity to be in the service of the Lord and experience the power of God with their own eyes. They are bold enough to walk up to him and ask, "So are you the one that is to come or shall we wait for another?"

They are bold enough to walk up to Jesus and ask Him, "Are you the one sent down through 40 and 2 generations or shall we wait for another?"

I appreciate the disciples and John for they were not just sitting around waiting for Jesus to show up. They were out serving tables! They didn't need the supervisor over their shoulders; they walked out by faith and worked their first work.

It teaches me to be mindful of people who have to see it to believe it. Sometimes, you have to believe it to see it. I appreciate people who have the guts to ask, "Are you the real thing or shall we wait for another?" Who are you? What are you doing? Do I have the right one, baby? Is that a Word from the Lord or shall we wait for another? Are you the right doctor, or shall we wait for another? Are you the Master Teacher or shall we keep on serving the Lord until the one comes who was and is to come?

And Jesus replied, "Go and tell John that this is the real deal and blessed are those who keep on moving in questionable times." Blessed are those who can send two to witness the ministry of another and not loose sight of the ministry they have. Jesus said, "Tell John do not stumble, but keep on moving."

John could have come himself but he was too busy saying, "I baptize you, in the name of the Father, in the name of the Son and in the name of the Holy Spirit."

The Bible records when they left, Jesus with the crowd in front of Him, paused the healing service to give John some kudos and to make a comparison and identify the children of fools from the children of wisdom.

Jesus asked which of them went to Wilderness Baptist Church to hear Brother John preach and got caught up in his outer appearance and the fact that he refused to indulge and received false prestige? Who in this audience went out to check out his outfit and missed his message? Which of you went out to check out his benefits and missed his benediction? Jesus said you went out just to hear some prophet, but he is more than a prophet!

Let me tell you John is a good man, and Flannery O'Connor says, "A good man, is hard to find."

John is the one the Bible calls the messenger who was sent before to let you know to get ready for my coming! Jesus says that John is the greatest born of a woman, but the Lamb slain for the sins of the world is greater than he. When Jesus tells us who John is, He also identifies Himself as the least in the kingdom of God.

This teaches us not to want a great seat in the house, but to desire the lowest seat. Don't look for the served seat; look for the servant's seat. Whoever is the greatest let him be the servant. For the servant will always get the reward of the house.

After understanding that John was really who he claimed to be, the crowd knew the message he preached really came from God.

Isn't it funny that the all the people gave God praise? Even the tax collectors, the rejects and despised in the community began to be thankful that they believed when they heard it and not when they saw it!

You've got to find people on your row that will believe it when they hear it and not just wait until they see it!

It was God's will for them to receive it by faith, not wait until Jesus got on the scene to confirm it.

Somebody needs to receive what God has said before you see it. Because if you believe it before you can see, you can guarantee that if God said it, He's going to do it. It will surely come to pass! Who are you? Whose child are you? Who's your daddy? If your Father said it, you can believe it! It will come to pass! Jesus says they believed and received it with baptism.

But wait a minute; those of you who refused to receive it with action, the Pharisees and the lawyers have rejected the plan of God for your life. Many people may have the law, but they don't have the plan. Many people have the constitution, but they don't have the big picture. Many people may have the instruction, but they may not have the idea. You may have the prescription, but may not know the purpose. You may have the warrant, but you may not have the way.

Matthew Henry comments,

"The Pharisees, who were most in reputation for religion and devotion, and the lawyers, who were celebrated for their learning, especially their knowledge of the Scriptures, rejected the counsel of God against themselves. They frustrated it; they

received the grace of God by the baptism of John in vain."

And if he is right, you can know the Bible backwards and forwards, but if you don't receive the salvific plan of God for your life, Jesus is forced to ask the question, whose child is this? Are you someone that is always coming up short, blocking their own blessing, shutting themselves out and excluding themselves? Who are these that are always trying to block and hinder somebody and always in somebody's way of receiving the plan of God for their life.

The question is raised in the hearing of the people, what shall I compare to the people of this generation and what are they like? It is here that Jesus helps us to identify any child.

Observe who they look like.

Who does this generation look like? Who do they resemble? These who refuse to repent? What is the craziest thing I can find to compare them to; Jesus says, "They look like children sitting in the marketplace calling one to another." We played the flute for you and you did not dance, we wailed, and you did not weep. Commentators state, "They are like those who fail to respond to all efforts to entice them to take part, whether it is a call to mourn or to dance."

And if they are right, this generation is like people who have many celebrations and they still do not respond.

Have you every tried to be positive and affirm your child and encourage them in every way possible and they still don't respond and change? That's what they look like. Have you come home and made the house ready for a mate and spiced up things and they still don't change? That's what they look like. Have you ever tried the no corporeal punishment and sat down and had a conversation and it still didn't work? That's what they look like. Have you ever tried to be up on time, show up on time, get ready in time and the supervisor never noticed? That's what they look like. Have you made every attempt to get their attention, changed your hair, lost weight, got some new teeth, and some new lips and they still never paid you attention? That's what they look like.

They look like children playing childhood games with a child that is too bossy, too stubborn, too mean, too selfish and knows too much to help themselves. Have you ever seen somebody that has gone through something that should have taken them out, and they still don't change? That's what they look like. Observe who they look like. Have you taken away every piece of entertainment, the iPod, the Internet, the cell phone, the car, the telephone and the credit card and that knuckle head still does not change? That's what they look like.

Have you taken your child to prison facilities, called the police, Montel Williams, nursing homes, children's hospitals and they still don't change? That's what they look like. Have you used the switch, the belt, power cords, the Frisbee, the tree limb and the uncle and they still don't change? That's what they look like. We played the wedding song for celebration and you still did not change. We played the funeral song for mourning and you shed not one tear. You better watch a child that does not cry when they get a whipping! The whippings don't work anymore. They are cold, they are angry, they are out of their minds and it is about to be on up in here! Observe who they look like.

Next Jesus says, "When John came on the scene, He did everything right, and lived right before you and was the example for you with humble lives. And I myself came and showed you how to sit and dine with sinners and not become a sinner. But you swore I had a demon because I was a friend to the outcasts."

Observe who they listen to.

John came and they did not listen and know Jesus Himself in their speaking and they refused to listen.

I have seen parents in the mall calling out to their children, "Billy, Billy, Billy, come here," and the child does not pay them any more attention than the hole in the wall. Observe who they listen to. A child knows who to listen to by the way you deal with them. If you play with them, they play with you. If you lie to them, they lie to you. If you step out on them, they step out on you. Observe who they listen to.

If you see Christ as your Chief Authority, you will follow His command. If you see the devil as your chief authority, you will follow his command. If you call their name and are right in their face, and they don't listen, you are not their authority! But some old gangbanger can tell them to do a drive by shooting and they do it, watch who they listen to. If the teacher says quiet three times and they still talk with disrespect, you are not the authority. If BET says, "Breath, stretch, shake and let it go," and you say come on, let's go, and they don't move, watch who they listen too. If somebody that does nothing for them gets all of their time and attention, watch who they listen to!

Here comes John with a message of life and hope and they refuse to listen. And Jesus says when you identify children you have to observe who they look like, and observe who they listen too, but you also have to watch what they do! Luke records, *"nevertheless wisdom is vindicated by all her children."*

Observe what they do.

I often watch how children act in the worship experience. When there are praising children, there is always a praising parent around to set the example. Wherever there is a praying child, there is always a praying parent around to set the example. Even if it is not a biological parent, there must be somebody who sets the example for the child to follow.

Even at McDonalds when I see hard working young people, I reckon there must have been some hard working somebody somewhere around to set the example for the child. And when I see lazy young people, there must be a lazy somebody somewhere around that set the example. Or a hardworking somebody who says it's okay to be lazy! If you need to identify a child, observe what they do. If a boy has enough nerve to hit a girl, he saw it somewhere that said it was okay to do so. If a child cusses out their parents, they saw somewhere that it was okay to do so. If a child spends all they got every time they get it, they saw somebody that set the example.

The song says, "Oh, be careful little hands what you do, for the Father up above is looking down in love." If a child is walking around dropping it like it's hot, they saw somebody else dropping it like it's hot. If you know the Superman and not the Son of Man it will show in what you do. If you know the Cupid Shuffle and not how to bind the Devil, it will show up in what you do. You have to watch what they do.

Who child is this? Whose child are you? Who's your baby daddy? Whose family do you come from? You better find out before you go any further! Even Jesus asked, *"Who is my mother and my brother, none but he that doth the will of my father?"* (Matthew 12:50 KJV) He asked the disciples, *"Who do people say that I am?"* (Matthew 16:13 NIV) Jesus raised the question, *"Why do you call me Lord, Lord, and do not practice what I tell you?"* (Luke 6:46) But Jesus, parenthetically, says, "Hold on, wait a minute." I can't worry about those who refuse my blessing. But wisdom, those who have the ability to hear my voice and do what I say, they are mine.

If they buy Starbucks for their enemies, they are mine. (Luke 6:27) Watch what they do. If they turn the other cheek, and walk away from a fight, they are mine. (Luke 6:29) If they give their resources, they are mine! (Luke 6:30) If they treat people right, they are mine! (Luke 6:31) If they love sinners, they are mine! (Luke 6:32) If they do good to haters, they are mine! (Luke 6:33) If they lend not to receive back, these are the children of the Highest! (Luke 6:35) If they are not merciful, whose child is this? If they are always judging, whose child is this? If they are not forgiving, whose child is that? If they write you off, whose child is that? That ain't God's child. It may be His creation, but it ain't His child! Whose child is this?

Luke 6:43 says, *"For a good tree bringeth not forth corrupt fruit; neither doth a corrupt tree bring forth good fruit. For every tree is known by the fruit it bears."* Jesus says, *"Those who hear my voice and obey my commands you can tell whose they are, by their life, their character and their deeds,"* (John 10:27) Whose child is this?

CHAPTER ELEVEN

How to Deal With Godly Growing Children

Focal Passage: Luke 2:41-52 (MSG)

41-45 Every year Jesus' parents traveled to Jerusalem for the Feast of Passover. When he was twelve-years-old, they went up as they always did for the Feast. When it was over and they left for home, the child Jesus stayed behind in Jerusalem, but his parents didn't know it. Thinking he was somewhere in the company of pilgrims, they journeyed for a whole day and then began looking for him among relatives and neighbors. When they didn't find him, they went back to Jerusalem looking for him. 46-48 The next day they found him in the temple seated among the teachers, listening to them and asking questions. The teachers were all quite taken with him, impressed with the sharpness of his answers. But his parents were not impressed; they were upset and hurt. His mother said, "Young man, why have you done this to us? Your father and I have been half out of our minds looking for you." ⁴⁹⁻⁵⁰ He said, "Why were you looking for me? Didn't you know that I had to be here, dealing with the things of my Father?" But they had no idea what he was talking about. ⁵¹⁻⁵² So he went back to Nazareth with them, and lived obediently with them. His mother held these things dearly, deep within herself. And Jesus matured, growing up in both body and spirit, blessed by both God and people.

They grow up so fast don't they? You know they didn't start out like this. From zero to 20-months-old, they are called "infants." At that age, they salivate over everything, eat, sleep and poop, and eat, sleep and poop; they even have coughing spells, but once they get our attention they stop.

Next from two to four-years-old, they are called "toddlers," and here they have temper tantrums, some entering and exiting the potty training stage, some start picking their noses and drinking bath water and some even eat the dog's food. In the middle of certain activities, they will stop what they are doing and start running around in circles, yelling at the top of their lungs, and then stop and go right back to what it was that they were doing. And toddlers know when they are pushing the limit.

Next from four to six-years-old, they are called

"preschoolers," and they run on their tippy toes and begin to skip. Here they sometimes have imaginary friends, and tend to brag and be very bossy. They are just now learning to take turns and share. And in this stage they also ask a lot of questions. Their language includes silly words and profanity, so you better not say or do anything in front of them that you are not willing to explain or confess.

Then from ages six to 13 we call them "school-aged," and by then they have smooth and strong motor skills. This is the age when peer acceptance becomes a priority. In this stage they have the ability to lie, steal and cheat. They learned how to negotiate the expectations and rules placed on them by family, friends, school and society.

School-aged children want to feel safe and should be involved in sports and learn how to function in traffic. Most parents like these years; for this is when the child can begin to engage in household chores like taking out the garbage and washing the dishes and vacuuming the floor. Oh, the joy of school-aged children. This is where they enter the stage called "adolescence," also known as "the threshold from childhood to adulthood; a transitional period whose chief purpose is the preparation of children for adult roles." They embrace the concept of individualization, with peer groups. And then from 13-14 years, they go through separation from their family. And oh man at age 15 to 17, they walk into a season of rebellion, but it's ok because they are trying to establish their identity. Around

18 and sometimes through 26, they come back to a place called "cooperation." This is where sometimes they get it and move out and start their own lives and families.

They just grow up so fast. However with all those stages of growth, there are some pivotal moments, some turning points that were sometimes the worst and at other times the best memories one could have when called to bring a child into this world, take on a child of another, already in this world, or simply participate in the growth process of the many children we encounter every day. I share with you these details as a type and shadow of the intentions of the Gospel writer Luke, whose aim is to provide a detailed account of the events in the life of Jesus, the Son of God, but also the Son of Man. Luke has a few concerns in his narrative discourse about the entering of God's Son into human history, the dates and details connecting Jesus and people in history, the deep interest Jesus had in people and relationships, the tender compassion and sympathy Jesus had for the poor and the dependence of Jesus to live under the guidance of the Holy Spirit.

Luke's story opens with the birth narratives containing the miracle birth of Jesus, which in itself causes major controversy for religious leaders and the contemporary believers of our day. He was born of the Holy Spirit, to a virgin engaged to a good, upstanding citizen of the community. Already the drama of the Lukan text unfolds for the arrival of Jesus is completely opposite of what the awaiting public was looking for.

The Messiah or Savior was supposed to come through the purest and most conventional of means. The Savior was supposed to be born on the tenth floor of the most prestigious hospital in the entire city, ushered in by the greatest pediatricians of that day, and not by some nervous husband, who was not able to make plans well in advance to get his wife a room in the Hilton, when they arrived to the festivals of celebration that everybody in the city attends every year. The Savior was not to be laid in a manger or trough filled with hay but in a Stork Craft Tuscany, 4-in-1 stages, baby crib in Espresso wrapped in a blanket purchased from the baby shower list, posted at Neiman Marcus. Already, the drama of Luke unfolds. And that is like our writer Luke, writing to a lover of God, a Theophilus, and a Roman audience possibly in the city of Caesarea about reversals.

Things are not what they seem. What you thought would end up one way for Luke turns out another. Who you thought would not be able to produce (Elizabeth) even in their old age, pushes out a John the Baptist. The one who should have said something (Zacharias) came out of the temple and the presence of God and says nothing. The one who should have been put away (Mary) ends up being loved and cherished by a man (Joseph) and even giving birth to the Son of God, who is also the Son of Man (Jesus).

This historical researcher writes to us about the reversals of life, the first shall be last and the last shall be first. The rich are made poor and the poor are made rich. The fatherless shall become a father and the motherless shall become a mother. The text is full of reversals, but also, turning points. You know, *turning points*, meaning "a decisive point at which a significant change or historical event occurs, or at which a decision must be made." Luke talks about crossroads, a place where one road crosses another. Crossroads are a place or an opportunity to change direction, change course, or change goals. It's good to read Luke, because somewhere in his message, Luke will encourage you to recognize that the moment of decision has arrived and it is time for you to either change direction, change course or change your goals.

Max Lemer puts it like this,

"The turning point in the process of growing up is when you discover the core of strength within you that survives all hurt."

And if he is right, if the hurt has come and gone and you are still alive, it is an indicator that this is your turning point. It is your opportunity to change direction, course or goal. Turning points are also known as pivotal moments in the growth process of our children's lives. And in our focal passage, the 12-year-old Son of God and Son of Man and His parents are at a climacteric moment, which Luke believes, but very few theological commentators suggest, warrant our attention.

In these verses, we have a historical account of how a family's religious obligation and tradition end up becoming a confrontation and criticism that encounters a compassionate

Christ, who is more concerned about the relationships He has forged than the prestige enthroned by the temple. This scene opens with parents who have a strong regard for the house of God and the ordinances of God. It begins with a group of parents who believe worldly matters come second to spiritual matters.

If you are going to be able to handle all that comes along with being an effective Godly influence of the life of any child, you must place the house of God and spiritual matters, above all worldly matters.

These parents teach us that there is some value in consistently making the journey to Jerusalem that will impact the lives of your children and yourselves.

Jesus had reached the age of 12, and in His culture, 12 is our modern day adolescence turned young adult, also known as the age where you begin to smell you self. In Hebrew culture, 12 to 13 was the time when young men began to take on adult responsibilities in the household of faith. It was a crossroads for the young man, an opportunity to change direction, change course and change goals. Here is our Jesus at the festival of the Passover, and for Him it became of importance to stay behind and hang out in the temple and attend to something that was of interest to Him. May I suggest that at some point in the life of our growing Godly children, something will become of importance to them that they may go after and be willing to stay behind for, that may not be on your agenda?

(There was a 4 year old young man names Dewayne Ham

Jr. also know as DJ? DJ is the son of Dewayne and Nikki Ham. A Sunday in 2009 after the celebration, DJ ran down to the front of the stage and got my attention to pick him up. I immediately assumed he wanted to give me a hug. SO I picked him up, but then he began to reach around me, and reached for the drumsticks and the drum set. So he jumped down and ran to the set, and began to play. He just used me to lift him up and right there the sermon for today started to develop).

If you are going to deal with these Godly-growing children, you might have to realize that their agenda and your agenda might change or reach a turning point. Back to the drama of the text, Jesus has decided to stay behind and His parents are unaware that He is not with them and that He is not in the caravan of friends and relatives. And the text says, *"When they could not find Him, they went back to Jerusalem to search for Him there."*

One day your children will do things and go places and you will not be able to find them. Now, they may be standing right in front of you, but you will not be able to find them.

So the wisdom that Mary and Joseph give to us is that when you can't find them, you might need to run back to Jerusalem. When you can't find them, even though they are standing right there in front of you, you might need to run back to the Holy City to search for them. Mary and Joseph did not know where their child was, but were confident that if they went back to the place of prayer and worship to seek Him, they would surely find their child.

Don't cuss at them; get back to the place of worship. Don't hit them in your anger; get back to the house of worship. Don't send them to the authorities or medicate them; get back to the house of worship.

Back to the drama of the text, and a little expository preaching: In verse 46, the text states that *"after three days they found him in the temple, sitting among the teachers listening to them and asking them questions."*

My first concern with this particular verse here is, why didn't anyone in the temple ask Jesus where his parents were? After all he'd been there questioning and listening for four days and they knew he was not there before the festival started. Surely someone in the temple wanted to know who he belonged to. Or were they so caught up in amazement with Him and with the 12-year-old grown man cultural tradition that they could not see He was still a boy? I believe Jesus was born in Africa, but this could not have been a black church. Or was it? In the traditional black church, you could not just show up for a few weeks and somebody not launch a full investigation of the "Five W's."

Who is it about? What happened? Where did it take place? When did it take place? Why did it happen? And how did it happen? Now that is the traditional black church. But nowadays, you can walk in the door, sit in the pew, read the text, eat the bread, drink the wine and walk right out and nobody will say anything to you, even children.

Why have we arrived to a place in the black church, where people can't say anything to our children when they are clearly out of the sight of their parents?

In verse 47, everyone in this setting is amazed with His understanding and His answers. What was He talking about, that amazed them so? You would think that since Luke thrives on giving a detailed account of the events, he would at least share with us some of the conversation. Or was the conversation not as important as the setting? Since the words were left out, maybe the actions of the characters without words are more important. And when everyone else is amazed with what is being said, we may want to stay focused with what is actually going on.

In verse 48, the teachers were all quite taken with Him, impressed with the sharpness of His answers. But His parents were not impressed; they were upset and hurt. When His parents saw him, they were astonished and His mother said, "Child why have you treated us like this? Look, your father and I have been searching for you in great anxiety."

A few concerns about the text. Did his parents have a choice to stick to amazement or move into inquisition? Why do some parents think that because their child is a wonder in public that they are not in need of correction right in the place of their wonder? Also, Mary begins the inquisition with Jesus. Isn't it culturally and traditionally accurate that when a boy reaches age 12, he is a man? Or is there a time to mother when a child is a child and engages in childlike actions that need to be corrected?

Both parents are present. Why did Joseph not take the lead in correction? He is the father, and after all, he is present. Could Joseph have been so angry that he felt it was best to not say anything at all? If so, could it be that our modern day fathers have gone silent when it comes to confronting their sons, or are they so hot tempered that they can't even express correction outside of aggression?

Why is Joseph quiet even after he fully participated in the search and has the same feelings of anxiety, grief and hopelessness, then when the boy is found, Joseph has nothing to say? I believe Jesus was born in Africa, but this could not have been a black man.

Is the silence of Joseph, representative of good fathering? If not, maybe God needs fathers who will not only participate in conception but also in compassionate correction?

In verse 48, His mother said, "Young man, why have you done this to us? Your father and I have been half out of our minds looking for you." Mary clearly expresses what Jesus' actions have done to them. He made them feel like they had been treated wrongly, and caused them great anxiety. She states, "Why have you treated us like this? Look, your father and I have been searching for you in great anxiety." Luke provides great details in saying that Joseph is standing at a distance, but Mary gets close to her son and confronts him. Is Mary pointing out the exhaustion of Joseph in his pursuit of Jesus? Is Mary trying to express, "Your father and I are tired of looking for you," the one we raised, the one we have cared for, the one we have shared the text with and the sacred scrolls with and been faithful to?

Look your father and I are tired of looking for you. We have walked the floor all night, and had no idea of where you were; we did not raise you like this. Now I believe Jesus was born in Africa, but I believe African American just showed up."

I can see the last 12 years of Jesus' life is brought into the conversation: Look here boy, we did not ask for you. An Angel showed up and the Holy Ghost dropped you off. This man was tricked into believing you were his Son, and even though you are not, he has taken care of you like you were his own. He agreed to stay with me even though he did not fully trust me. He has taken the grunt of this situation and every year taken you and your brothers and sisters on family vacations, and been there to teach you a trade and start a business for you to carry on. He has given you an earthly inheritance. If it was not for those three shepherds showing up in the field that night and bringing gifts and his having the wisdom to manage what they brought, we would have been out on the streets. And here we are doing what we have always done for the church and the family, and we leave and you stay behind and not tell us.

We have been searching for you for days, I know you're grown, but you aren't that grown. And everybody else might be amazed, but I'm your mother and I can smell the stank and know it's stank. Your father and I are tired of looking for you. Where are the values we taught you? Where are the morals, and rules we shared with you? You know not to go off with strangers. You know to stay close to the family. You know not to cross the street when danger is present. We taught you to always let us know where you are going. We taught you to always come to us if you have a problem or a concern or if you wanted to do something.

We thought we failed, even though we gave you our best and we have tried and tried. We have been searching for three days. Do you know what can happen in three days?

You can go to hell and back in three days. If you don't sleep for three days you can loose mental composure from sleep deprivation and become an insomniac. In three days the body is halfway into starvation mode if you don't feed it. If you don't sleep for three days you will begin to hallucinate, and see things that are not really there. If you don't sleep for three days you will not be able to think clearly and make rational choices. If you lived under government housing you can be put out in three days. Here it is three days later and possibly, our thinking has been off, our eyesight has been blurred, we have not slept, our bodies have gone into starvation and your father and I are tired of looking for you.

In verse 49, Jesus responds, "Why are you searching for me? Did you not know that I must be in my Father's house?

Is it that, in Jesus' understanding He feels that He was right in what He was doing? According to their culture He was of age and able to make those decisions and not have to report to someone. Or is this response more meaningful? In verse 50, it is stated that they did not make the connection between Jesus being in and concerned with His heavenly Father's house and returning to His earthly father's house and its business. Why so? In verse 51, Jesus left the temple and went with His parents to Nazareth and the text explicitly says "and was obedient to them."

In contemporary culture, is it that, at some point you have to trust that you have deposited enough into your children, that when you question them about what you feel has been a mistreatment to who you are and what you have taught them that they will come down from where they are, and come back to obedience? Don't allow your children to do things without questioning them. I would even almost suggest that you launch an investigation into their daily lives and activities.

Jesus here does the most amazing thing. He not only announces His divinity, but He also actualizes His humanity. He is concerned with His heavenly Father's agenda, but He is also concerned with His earthly father's heart.

About the Author

Reverend Willie J. Thompson, Jr. affectionately known as Pastor Willie, was born and raised in Columbia, South Carolina.

After receiving his Baccalaureate Degree in Religion and Philosophy from Benedict College in Columbia, South Carolina and his Masters of Divinity Degree from Howard University in Washington, D.C., Reverend Thompson is currently completing his PhD in Sociology at Howard University. In 2013, the Board of Trustees of the School of the Great Commission, with endorsements from the Georgia Bible Institute and the Triune Professional Association of Richmond, Virginia, conferred upon Reverend Thompson, the Honorary Degree of Doctor of Divinity.

Pastor Willie served as the youth and young adult pastor of Prince George's Community Presbyterian Church (Bowie, MD) and Oak Grove Baptist Church (Elgin, SC) from 2005 until

2012 and now serves as Senior Pastor, at Morning Star Baptist Church in Clairton, PA. Pastor Willie has a dynamic preaching and teaching ministry. His relevant presentation of the Gospel will inspire and motivate you to be all God has called you to be. He is passionate about the Cause of Christ, consumed with seeing people come into relationship with Jesus and committed to championing the cause of the global church.

Pastor Willie attributes his earthly success to his many God-given spiritual fathers and mothers. His heart and passion is to build real, open and honest relationships reaching people, by any means necessary, with the life changing truth found in Jesus Christ. To this end, he travels worldwide, ministering the liberating Word of God.

Pastor Willie has been dubbed a present-day "David" because of his zealous passion for true praise and worship. He is an anointed leader, who has become a man after God's own heart.

Need
additional
copies?

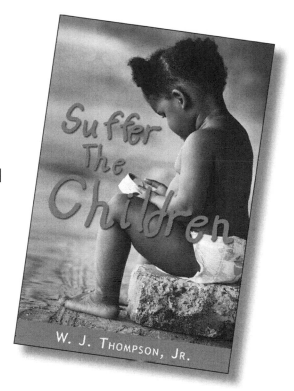

To order more copies of

Suffer The Children

contact CertaPublishing.com

❒   Order online at:
     CertaPublishing.com/Bookstore

❒   Call 855-77-CERTA or

❒   Email Info@CertaPublishing.com